*Then you will know the truth, and the
truth will set you free.*

—JOHN 8:32 (NIV)

Under the Apple Tree
As Time Goes By
We'll Meet Again
Till Then
I'll Be Seeing You
Fools Rush In
Let It Snow
Accentuate the Positive
For Sentimental Reasons
That's My Baby
A String of Pearls
Somewhere Over the Rainbow

WHISTLE STOP
Café
= MYSTERIES =

SOMEWHERE OVER the RAINBOW

LAURA BRADFORD

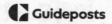

Guideposts

Whistle Stop Café Mysteries is a trademark of Guideposts.

Published by Guideposts
100 Reserve Road, Suite E200
Danbury, CT 06810
Guideposts.org

Cover and interior design by Müllerhaus
Cover illustration by Greg Copeland at Illustration Online LLC.
Typeset by Aptara, Inc.

ISBN 978-1-961126-62-6 (hardcover)
ISBN 978-1-961126-63-3 (epub)

Printed and bound in the United States of America
10 9 8 7 6 5 4 3 2 1

SOMEWHERE OVER the RAINBOW

CHAPTER ONE

*J*anet Shaw moved between tables with a lightness that had nothing to do with the lilac-scented May air wafting through the open café windows or the high praise her new peach pie had earned from her regulars. No, this lightness, this joy, was about something a million times better. Something she'd been waiting for since mid-January when—

"Oh." Janet stopped, gazed over a customer's shoulder, and took in the sketch gracing the bottom two-thirds of a napkin that bore the café's logo. "Did you draw that?"

The gray-haired newcomer set her pencil down and pushed the napkin into the center of the table. "I did, but it's nothing. Just a house I glimpsed through some trees this morning. It was a fast glance, though, so I improvised a lot. And not terribly well, I'm afraid."

Janet took in the cottage-like house, the flowers lining what appeared to be a slate walkway, and the pair of cozy rockers on the front porch that made her yearn to sit in one and watch the day go by. "Are you kidding me? It's beautiful. How long have you been drawing like that?"

"If my mother were still alive, she'd say that I've spent far too much of my life doodling on paper, napkins, sticky notes, and anything else I could find. But my fingers can't seem to stop themselves sometimes. It's what I do. What I've always done."

Janet stepped around the side of the table to speak with the woman more easily. "I've been doodling my whole life. And that"—she indicated the napkin—"is most definitely not doodling."

"You're too kind." The woman pointed at her empty plate and then smiled up at Janet. "I have to say, that chocolate cream pie might very well be the best I've ever had. And I've had a lot over the years. Is it exclusively a Saturday offering?"

"I'm glad you enjoyed it, and no, it's a regular on our menu."

"Good to know." The woman's gaze dropped from Janet's. "I like your shirt."

Janet looked down at the bold white lettering that ran across her chest—I Bake, Therefore I Am—and laughed. Usually, her punny T-shirts were covered by her apron, but this was a special one she'd wanted to show off to the café crowd. "Thank you. My daughter, Tiffany, found it for me in a shop not far from her college and gave it to me last night."

Then, unable to hold back her happiness, Janet lowered herself onto the edge of the vacant chair across from the woman. "She officially completed her first year at Case Western Reserve University in Cleveland yesterday, and I'm beyond thrilled at having her home with me for the entire summer. When she's not working or hanging out with her friends, that is."

"I see. The humming makes sense now."

"I was humming?" Janet asked.

The woman nodded, smiling. "Your girl is back in the nest again. It makes sense."

"Back in the nest. I like that." Janet extended her hand to the woman with a grin. "I'm Janet Shaw. My friend Debbie Albright and I own this café."

"I'm Audrey Barker, Dennison's newest resident, according to my real estate agent."

"How wonderful. Welcome! You're going to love it here—I just know it."

"That's music to my ears. Thank you."

"What brings you to Dennison?" Janet asked. "Do you have family here?"

Audrey's smile dimmed momentarily. "No, I'm the last of the Barkers, I'm afraid. But I needed to downsize, and I wanted to stay in Ohio. When I did a little research on towns in this county, Dennison really stood out to me."

"I take it you're a history buff?" Janet prodded.

"I don't know if I qualify as a history buff, per se, but Dennison's—and this depot's—ties to World War II intrigue me." Audrey ran the tip of her index finger around the rim of her empty coffee mug. "My father often spoke about coming through this very depot on his way to war. He talked of the townspeople and the kindness they showed him and the other soldiers."

"That's wonderful," Janet said. "When you have time, I highly encourage you to check out the museum at the other end of the building. Kim Smith, the curator, has a wealth of information regarding the station and the service members it served. In fact, Kim's mother, Eileen Palmer, actually stepped in as stationmaster during the Second World War and is still living right here in Dennison."

Audrey leaned forward, intrigued. "How fascinating."

"It truly is. Kim does an amazing job making history come to life for visitors," Janet said. "I could go on and on, but suffice it to say that you've picked a wonderful place to call home, Audrey. The kindness your father spoke about is still very much alive and well in this town. It really is."

"And a person can get a *very* nice piece of chocolate cream pie here every day of the week," Audrey said with a chuckle.

"Every day but Sunday," Janet corrected.

"Of course. Sunday is the Lord's Day." Audrey tapped her empty plate. "But knowing it's here the other six days of the week will be a nice carrot—and, at times, a solace—as I get settled in my new home."

Janet crossed one leg over the other. "What do you need a carrot for?"

"I engaged in far too much procrastination in the weeks leading up to my move. As a result, the failure to pare down my belongings *before* I got here has resulted in the need for a storage unit I'd rather not continue to pay for. Thus, your pie will serve as my carrot to finally go through everything once and for all. I'll allow myself a piece only on days that I've made some progress emptying the unit."

"And the solace?"

Audrey's eyes filled with tears. "Much of what's in that storage unit belonged to my mother. She passed two years ago at the age of ninety-seven."

"I'm sorry for your loss."

"Thank you," Audrey said, recovering. "I'll be donating most of her books to the local library, and her clothes to any women's shelters in the area, but I need to go through the rest of her things and decide what to keep."

"Naturally. It's good that you have a plan."

"Yes, that helps, but the whole task still feels overwhelming. Makes me wish I had a fairy godmother who could drop down from the sky and do all the sorting for me." Audrey stretched, and kneaded her lower back. "If left to my own devices, I'll hem and haw over every little item, no matter how inconsequential it might be."

Janet considered the woman's words. "I'm sure you could probably find someone to do that for you. Maybe a college kid home for…" The words faded from her lips as her thoughts caught up to her mouth.

"Is your daughter looking for work?" Audrey asked, her eyes widening. "Because I'll pay, and I'll pay well if she is."

"Actually, she's fairly free right now," Janet said. "She has a standing job as a lifeguard every summer, starting in June. And the only thing I need her for is to help me plan her father's birthday party at the end of the month."

"Well, if she would like the job, here's my contact info." Audrey wrote her name and phone number across the bottom of the penciled sketch and offered it to Janet. "It's only fifteen—maybe twenty—boxes at most. I don't think it would take her much more than a day or so to go through them all. And, as I said, I'll pay well."

"When were you thinking?" Janet asked.

Audrey's shoulders hiked upward. "Sometime this coming week? Monday would be great."

"I'll talk to Tiffany about it at dinner tonight."

"Thank you." Audrey slid her pencil into her handbag and stood. "Though, if she agrees to help, I'll be forced to come up with another reason to treat myself to a piece of your chocolate cream pie on occasion."

Janet rose as well, her gaze lifting from the drawing to the woman responsible for it. "The way I see it, Audrey, there should be no occasion necessary when it comes to pie. Or cookies. Or cake. Or brownies. Or really any baked item, for that matter."

"Then I'll come just because."

Janet tucked the napkin into her pocket and smiled. "Sounds like the perfect reason to me."

CHAPTER TWO

$\mathcal{S}$lowly but surely, they were making progress. Books were stacked in piles to their left, and clothes had been sorted into bins labeled DONATE and RECYCLE to their right. And scattered about between the two were the contents of one of the last boxes.

"You didn't need to take the day off to do this with me, Mom." Tiffany's green eyes met Janet's. "Miss Barker hired *me* to go through this stuff, not you."

Waving away her daughter's words with one hand, Janet added a winter hat to the donation bin with the other. "Need I remind you that other than your birthday weekend in March, you haven't been home since your winter break?"

"No, I'm aware."

"Well then, if going through boxes is the way to sneak in time with you, I'll go through boxes."

Tiffany's answering laugh brought a smile to Janet's lips. "You can't fool me. I know you couldn't have taken today off on a whim. You had to have baked like crazy last week to be able to be with me today. So I've deduced that you'd already planned to take today off. You just didn't know we'd be doing this."

"You are too smart for your own good." Janet pulled her lavender T-shirt away from herself to display the various smudges and marks earned over the past few hours. "There's nothing I'd rather be doing right now."

"You're crazy, Mom."

"About you? Guilty as charged." Taking in the smattering of knickknacks lined up in front of Tiffany, Janet pointed at the last two unopened boxes. At her daughter's answering nod, she retrieved one and then sat back down on the step stool she'd commandeered as a makeshift chair. "So...I'm at a total loss on what to get your father for his birthday."

Tiffany returned to sorting the objects from the box she was going through. She rotated a figurine, inspecting it for cracks, then gently set it aside. "Just regift one of the things you've given him in the past that he never opened. He'll never know."

"Tiffany Arabella Shaw, I can't do that!"

Her daughter raised an eyebrow at her. "Have you been in the attic recently, Mom? You absolutely could."

Janet tsked softly under her breath as she read the label written in marker across the top of the cardboard box on the floor in front of her. MAMA'S THINGS. "Your father isn't a materialistic person, Tiffany. You know that."

"You're right. I do. Yet, every year, like clockwork, you ask him what he wants, and he tells you a blueberry pie or a double-chocolate cake or an apple turnover. And what do you do? You get him a new tool or a model airplane kit or something else he'll never take out of the box." Tiffany blew an errant strand of dark red hair off her freckled cheek and moved on to pairing gloves. "So how about you *don't* get him something this year, Mom? Wrap up one of your pies, and he'll be beyond thrilled."

"I can't give your father a pie for his birthday."

"But if it's what makes him happiest, why not?"

Janet's shoulders sagged. "I don't know. It's just not good enough."

"It would be for Dad."

"He deserves to feel more celebrated than that though. He's such a special man." Janet grabbed the box cutter and carefully slid the blade through the tape.

Tiffany stood, added her latest empty box to the pile of other empty boxes, and stretched, her chin quivering with a quiet yawn. "I'll think about it then. But no guaran—wait!"

Janet jerked her gaze from the pile of papers inside her own box to her daughter. "You have an idea already?"

"We could do one of those genealogy things for him so he could learn more about his Scottish ancestors."

She considered her daughter's words. "That could be fun—a *lot* of fun, in fact. But I don't think we could get it back before the party. There's no telling how long that would take."

"Didn't Debbie's dad get some sort of test like that done faster when his sister suspected she was adopted?" Tiffany asked.

"It was a DNA test, but yes. And they weren't trying to trace their DNA over generations, which takes a couple of months. They were only checking whether the two of them were biologically related." Returning her focus to the box, Janet sifted through the top layer of yellowing notepads and journals. "Tracing ancestry would probably take a bit longer than we have. This year, anyway."

"You're probably right." Tiffany returned to their work area, peeked inside Janet's latest box, and sat down opposite her. "I think I need a break from clothes and knickknacks for a while."

Janet plucked out a few items and pushed the box of notepads toward Tiffany. "So what did Audrey say about sorting her mother's papers?"

"She asked me to organize them so she can go through them once the donation stuff is outta here." Rising to her knees, Tiffany reached inside the box, pulled out a pile of papers, and sucked in a breath. "Hey, I recognize this. It's one of my favorites."

Glancing up from the notepad in her hand, Janet asked, "What did you find?"

"This drawing." Tiffany held up a sketch of a young woman sporting a white T-shirt and braids holding a pail of strawberries. "It's a still from one of the animated shorts I learned about in my History of Film elective last semester. They came out during World War II. Some were created for the public to boost morale. Others were for educating and training the troops. This one"—Tiffany held the page higher—"was to inspire civilians to support the war effort by growing their own food instead of getting everything from the store."

Tiffany handed the paper to Janet and then dropped her attention back to her lap and the remaining pile stacked there. "Oh, this is the next cel. Or, rather, the next drawing that would become a cel."

"A cel?" Janet echoed.

"Yeah—that's a piece of flexible plastic used in 2D animation. Each cel has a drawing outlined on one side, and the colors are filled in on the other side. Then the cels are placed over a background and photographed in story sequence. The movement, or illusion of movement, comes from playing them back at a certain speed."

"But this isn't plastic," Janet said, holding up the drawing of the girl with the strawberries.

"Before computers, the artwork was done by hand on paper first and then transferred onto a cel. See this one?" Tiffany held up another drawing—one of the same woman in the process of picking a strawberry. "This came before the one you have." Tiffany flipped through a few of the pages on her lap. "They're out of order from what I remember Dr. Carter showing us, but I think they're all here."

"Dr. Carter was your professor?"

Tiffany nodded. "He was awesome, Mom. He made everything we learned come alive. I'm probably biased toward World War II history because of growing up in a town like Dennison, but the section on animation during the war was really cool. The shorts aimed at people on the home front were some of the more interesting ones for me, and this one"—she pointed at the drawing in her hand—"was my favorite of the bunch."

"What do you think it is about that one that appeals to you so much?" Janet asked.

"I love how it was aimed at women and showed a simple way that they could help with the war effort, even far out in the country," Tiffany said. "I mean, we know women did a lot to keep the country running and to support the soldiers by working in factories, driving streetcars, and stuff like that. But lots of other women helped in ways hardly anybody talks about. This woman is growing food for herself and her neighbors."

"Are there enough pages in the box to show how the short went?" Janet asked.

Tiffany retrieved the strawberry-picking picture from Janet, slid it into a pile she painstakingly ordered, and then held it up for

Janet to see while she flipped through it. As she did, Janet was able to imagine how it might have played out on a screen.

"Wow," she said with a smile.

Tiffany stilled the papers. "The guy who did this piece was Kenneth Hartman. The rest of his work was geared more toward soldiers. Those animated shorts were about weapons, training techniques, and the enemy. They were well done, but I prefer his work on this one." Tiffany flipped through the pictures one more time and then placed the pile in her lap. "The others—the ones for the soldiers—were kind of depressing. But this one, with the woman, the farm, the little boy peeking through the slats of the fence in the hope of landing a strawberry at the end... I felt *hope* after I watched it, instead of fear."

Janet reached into the box for yet another pile of papers. "I can see why you'd be drawn to that one," she said, glancing back up at her daughter. "I'm really glad you enjoyed your class so much."

"I pretty much liked all my classes, but Dr. Carter's class was a fun one. I'm glad I took it. But as much as I loved the short these drawings are done from, I can't imagine taking the time or the effort to copy all the cels from it."

Janet sifted through the papers in her own lap and started a pile for photographs. "I try to recreate things we eat in restaurants, right?"

"You do."

"And I try to figure out dishes I hear people gushing about, right?"

"Where are you going with this, Mom?"

"Audrey drove by a cottage yesterday and then took the time to draw it on a napkin between bites of pie and sips of coffee," Janet said. "So I don't find it at all far-fetched to think she'd draw other things that struck her fancy throughout her life."

"You think Miss Barker drew these?" Tiffany asked, her eyes wide.

Janet shrugged. "It's what makes sense to me."

"But they're in a box of her mother's things."

"You don't think I kept that project you did on the heart for your fifth-grade science fair?" Janet asked. "Or the one you did in high school on the importance of hydration?"

Tiffany's mouth gaped. "You did?"

"Of course I did." Janet added a few photographs to the pile and then abandoned them in favor of her daughter. "You spent so much time on them, and we were proud of your work. How could I *not* keep them?"

Tiffany's gaze dropped to the stack of drawings in her lap. "These are way better than either of those projects."

"Not to me they're not." Janet grabbed another pile from the box. "But it's nice that her mother saved them." She sorted the last stack of papers into their appropriate piles and blew out a slow, deliberate breath. "I got the sense that Audrey's mother didn't put much stock in her talent. Like she didn't want to encourage it if she didn't believe it could go somewhere. Which, sadly, is probably why Audrey doesn't believe it could either."

Tiffany placed the pile of drawings on the floor beside the photographs. "That's too bad," she said. "You and Dad have always been my biggest cheerleaders."

For a long moment, Tiffany thumbed back through the artwork. Then she got up. "Maybe if Miss Barker knew her mother saved these sketches, it would help her believe in her talent."

"Maybe." Janet rose and dusted off her jeans.

"Can I be the one to tell her?" Tiffany asked.

"You're the one she hired to go through these boxes, aren't you?"

Tiffany smiled. "Yes. But you're here too."

"True. But for an entirely different reason than you are." She gave her daughter a pointed look.

"I gave you my thoughts on Dad's birthday present," Tiffany said. "It's up to you whether you listen or not."

Janet laughed. "That's not why I'm here, and you know it."

"You *don't* want my help with Dad's party?" Tiffany teased.

Crossing her arms in front of her chest, Janet glowered at her. "Of course I do."

Tiffany's laugh hung in the air, and she gave Janet a hug. "We'll have time together this summer, Mom. I promise."

"You better be careful with a statement like that, because I'll hold you to it."

"Good." Tiffany checked something on her phone then swooped down to retrieve the drawings. "Now let's go get some lunch."

CHAPTER THREE

'd say I'm surprised to see you, Janet, but I'm not. Can't even stay away on your day off, can you?" Debbie settled herself onto the countertop stool to the left of Tiffany and swiveled to face them. "There are other places to go for lunch in and around Dennison, ladies."

Tiffany glanced from Debbie to her mom with a grin. "Oh, it gets better, Debbie. Do you want to know how Mom spent her entire morning on her supposed day off?"

"Hmm." Debbie's brown eyes rolled playfully toward the ceiling as she made a show of thinking about it. "Trying new recipes?"

Tiffany shook her head.

"Making cookies or brownies or some other treat for the guys at the police department?"

"Nope."

"Cleaning and organizing her pantry?"

"Nope."

"Shopping online for more baking-themed T-shirts to add to her collection?"

Tiffany's laugh stirred a matching one from Debbie. "No."

"Okay, okay." Janet held up her hands. "You can both stop having fun at my expense now."

Debbie glanced around Tiffany for a better view of Janet and grinned at her. Then she said, "I'm out of guesses."

"She's been opening boxes and sorting all kinds of stuff at a storage area on the other side of town. A storage area that *I* was hired to go through. On my own. Which I was more than capable of doing."

Janet rested her chin on her hand. "If that's what I needed to do to spend time with my daughter, so be it."

Debbie reached around Tiffany to pat Janet's shoulder. "And here I was, making fun of you."

Scrunching her nose, Tiffany pushed away her nearly empty glass of iced tea. "You did hear what I said, right? She spent her day off going through boxes that were *my* responsibility. Not hers."

"I heard. But I've also been listening to your mom since the day you went back to school after your winter break. In fact, there was a countdown calendar for your return on the wall in the kitchen, and it's why she took today off—so she could spend it with you."

Tiffany flashed a smile at Janet. "A countdown calendar? Like we used to make for trips and stuff when I was little?"

"Yes." Janet smiled back at her. "Having you home again—even for a few months—is better than any trip in my book. Unless you're on the trip too, of course."

"Thanks, Mom. Like I told you, I figured out today was a planned day off, but I didn't know you had something special for us to do today. If I had, I wouldn't have accepted the storage cleaning gig. Or I would've done it another day."

"Nonsense. We were together at the storage area, and we're together now. As far as I'm concerned, it's a perfect day." Janet smiled at Debbie. "Has it been busy around here this morning?"

"Busy enough, but not so much that Paulette and I can't handle it." Debbie slid off the stool and pointed at the manila folder beside Janet's sandwich plate. "Do you want me to put that somewhere?"

Janet laid a hand on the folder. "Actually, that's something Tiffany found in one of the boxes this morning. She thinks Audrey Barker might like to see it."

"Audrey Barker," Debbie repeated. "Do I know that name?"

"She's the woman I met here on Saturday. She drew that cottage on the napkin I showed you after she'd left."

"Right. I remember now," Debbie said. "That was a really good picture. I wanted to step into that cottage the moment you showed it to me."

"And that's apparently the tip of the iceberg when it comes to her talent," Janet said, motioning toward the folder. "A talent she is clearly far too quick to dismiss, right, Tiffany?"

Tiffany opened her mouth to answer but closed it again as the front door of the café swung open. Audrey stepped inside and scanned the tables and chairs.

Janet waved her over then slid off her stool to welcome her with a warm hug. "Audrey, hello. Thanks for agreeing to meet us here, especially on such short notice. This is my daughter, Tiffany."

Audrey shook Tiffany's hand and smiled. "I'm glad to put a face with your voice on the phone. I trust the manager gave you access to my storage unit as I requested this morning?"

"He did."

"Wonderful. And since you're not running for the back door at the sight of me, I'm guessing it's safe to assume it wasn't too horrible a task to go through those boxes?"

Tiffany grinned. "Not horrible at all, Miss Barker. In fact, Mom came along with me. It gave us lots of time to talk."

"That's nice. Now, Tiffany, call me Audrey, please. Were you able to sort things out pretty well?"

"Yes. There's a pile of books for the library, a few bins of clothing for the women's shelter, a recycling bin, and a trash pile." Tiffany perched on the edge of her stool. "I can go with you when you check through it all, and once you're sure everything's been sorted right, I'll take stuff to the library and the women's shelter for you. And to the dump and recycling too."

"That would be lovely, my dear. Thank you."

Janet finished the introductions. "Audrey, this is my best friend and my co-owner here at the Whistle Stop, Debbie Albright. Debbie, this is Dennison's newest resident, Audrey Barker."

"Welcome to Dennison, Audrey. We're glad to have you." Debbie released Audrey's hand. "I should get back to work, but how about the three of you move over to one of the tables, where you'll be more comfortable?"

Janet took in the line of stools and the handful of unoccupied tables. "I think that's a great idea. How about that table over in the corner?"

Audrey and Tiffany agreed, so Janet led the way to the quiet table. When they were seated, Debbie handed Audrey a menu and recommended a few of the most popular dessert items. After Audrey placed her order, Janet motioned to Tiffany to take the lead on the conversation.

"We sorted all but one box." Tiffany ran her finger over the folder she'd placed on the table. "There are some things we went through you'll probably want to throw away, but I didn't feel comfortable making that call before you saw everything."

"I appreciate that," Audrey said.

"The last box we opened held mostly notebooks and mementos of your mom's, so I did a little organizing. The other was marked 'Personal Papers,' so I didn't touch that one at all. For obvious reasons."

"Outstanding, dear, thank you." Audrey leaned back in her chair. "My mom was my best friend my entire life. Losing her truly upended my whole world. She knew everything about me, and I knew everything about her, so going through her things shouldn't be so difficult. Yet every time I convince myself it's time to do so, I chicken out. I guess the mere thought of handling her letters and papers brings a level of finality I'm not ready for. I don't know when I will be ready, to be honest. Perhaps in my new house, instead of seeing it as something final, I can see it as a little visit of sorts. Her touch in my new life."

"Tell us about her," Janet said.

Emotion shimmered in Audrey's blue-gray eyes. "Her name was Suzannah Mae Barker, but everyone called her Mae. She was born and raised on a farm with four older brothers, spending the bulk of her time cooking, cleaning, and baking alongside my grandmother while her father and brothers tended to the animals and the crops."

"That couldn't have been easy," Janet murmured.

"When she married my father, her entire world was our home— making sure it was clean, the meals were healthy, and my brother and I stayed on the straight and narrow so that we too would have a good, solid life. And she succeeded. My brother worked his way to the top spot in his New York City accounting firm before his death ten years ago. And a little over five years ago, I retired from the nursing career she always wanted me to have, enabling us to travel together before her health made getting around too difficult."

Tiffany's chair legs scraped against the floor as she scooted closer to the table. "Mom showed me the cottage you drew on the napkin. It's really, really good. I love the detail and the shading."

Audrey's cheeks flushed pink with praise she was quick to wave away. "Thank you. You're too kind. But it's like I told your mom. I'm simply a doodler. When I was a girl, I doodled in school. I doodled at work when my coworkers were repeating the same stories I'd been hearing for years. And I still tend to doodle, especially when I'm eating out, as I did here the other day. Next to my mom, paper and a pencil have always been my closest friends."

"Did you ever think about pursuing art as a career path instead of nursing?" Tiffany asked.

"In my dreams, sure." Audrey smiled as Paulette placed a piece of chocolate cream pie in front of her with a cup of coffee. "I imagined being a children's book illustrator, an art teacher, a famous artist with gallery showings in Italy—the whole nine yards. But it wasn't practical or realistic."

"But you're *good*."

Audrey took a bite of pie. "You're sweet, dear. Truly. But things are different for your generation than they were for mine. In my day, women could become teachers, nurses, and secretaries but not much more. And when they got married, they usually quit so they could run a household and raise children. I considered teaching for a little while but opted for nursing instead, with my mom's encouragement."

"But women made such huge strides in the workforce during World War II, right?" Tiffany said. "Why did they give that all up when the war was over?"

Audrey traded a smile with Janet across the top of her coffee cup. "Do you want to take this, Mom, or should I?"

"I've got it." Janet turned to her daughter. "They 'gave it up,' as you say, *because* the war was over. The jobs they had went back to the men who returned home."

Tiffany studied the chocolate chip cookie she'd ordered while Audrey and Janet took sips of their drinks. "That doesn't seem fair," she said.

"It's just the way it was." Audrey set her cup down. "It was different back then. Time moves on. Things change."

"Education and new opportunities made it so it could be different for me"—Janet spread her arms wide to indicate the café—"and even more so for your generation."

Tiffany looked up. "I'm glad of that," she said with a grin.

"What do you want to do with your future, Tiffany?" Audrey asked.

Tiffany broke off a piece of her cookie. "I'm not a hundred percent sure yet, but I'm mostly interested in math and science. Maybe something in the medical or pharmaceutical world. I've been taking different types of courses to figure it out."

"You just finished your freshmen year of college, right?" At Tiffany's nod, Audrey continued. "Then you have time to figure it out. In the meantime, though, soak it all up. Enjoy your youth. Full-blown adulthood will be here before you know it."

Tiffany returned the uneaten portion of her cookie to her plate and met Audrey's gaze. "It's not too late, you know."

"Too late for what?" Audrey asked.

"To have that gallery showing. Or to illustrate a kids' book. Or to teach an art class." Tiffany leaned forward. "One of my college professors must be close to your age, and he just started teaching a couple of years ago. He's really passionate about the subjects he teaches."

Audrey laughed. "That's wonderful, Tiffany, but I'm not an artist. I can practically hear my mother rolling in her grave at the thought of me traveling down that path. 'Time isn't meant to be wasted on frivolity,' she always said."

"But it's not a waste of time if you're good at it," Tiffany insisted, pushing her plate to the side. "And you are. You're really good."

"I'm seventy-one, young lady."

"That's not so old," Tiffany said. And isn't 'better late than never' a thing for a reason?"

"For some people, I suppose. But my time and effort are best spent on something 'real,' as my mother always said." Audrey finished the last of her pie. "Which currently means getting my new place in order and making time to go through the two boxes you set aside. After that, it will mean getting to know my new community, planting a garden in my backyard, and finding places to volunteer where my nursing background can be of assistance."

Janet smiled at her. "I suspect your mother was prouder of you and your artwork than you realize."

Audrey returned her smile. "I have no doubt my mother was proud of me. She wore my time as a nurse like a badge of honor.

But as far as my incessant doodling on every piece of paper, napkin, receipt, and anything else I could reach, 'tolerated' would be a more accurate description."

"Tiffany, would you like to show Audrey what we found?"

Tiffany slid the folder across the table to Audrey. "I don't think your mom would've saved these if she wasn't proud of your talent. By the way, they're amazing. I loved that short film too."

Audrey's confused expression gave way to curiosity as she took the folder and slowly opened it. "What is this?" she asked, dividing her attention between her tablemates and the drawings.

Janet tilted her head. "Aren't they yours? They're based on an animated short film from World War II."

"I've never seen these before," Audrey replied. "Where did you get them?"

"They were in one of the boxes in your storage area," Tiffany said. "One marked 'Mama's Things.'"

"They were?" Audrey flipped through the drawings, her face pinched. "I don't understand."

"You labeled the box," Janet reminded her.

Audrey thumbed to the next picture. "I did, but like I told you, I didn't go through the boxes. I just looked inside to see what kinds of things they were and then put labels on them."

"You didn't go through any of it?" Tiffany asked.

"No. I couldn't. Not in her old house, where her presence was still so strong." Audrey examined the last drawing and then slowly studied each one again, in reverse order. "She never showed me any of these, and she showed me everything. We both did. We were best friends."

Janet watched her, unsure how to ease her new friend's mind.

When she reached the top drawing again, Audrey raised her head, and the bewilderment she felt was evident on her face. "You said something about these being from World War II?"

"Yes," Tiffany said. "They're drawings from an animated short film that was shown here in the States during the war." She repeated the explanation she'd given Janet about the short.

"Okay, but how did they end up in my mother's things?" Audrey asked.

Janet finished her drink and folded her hands in her lap. "We assumed, based on your obvious talent, that you'd drawn them at some point and she'd saved them, as mothers often do."

"But I didn't."

"Is there any chance she drew them?" Janet asked. "Since they were in with her things?"

Audrey's laugh echoed around them. "My mother? Drawing?" Without waiting for an answer, she held up the top paper. "Even if she'd exhibited any interest in it, do you know the kind of time that went into drawing something with this much detail? And then to go on and do this many, all with the same level of detail?" She held up the rest of the stack. "No. My mother spent every moment of her life doing what she was supposed to do. Cooking, cleaning, canning, caring for my father, raising us kids, and steering us toward real careers. She had no use for drawing. Not for her, and not for me."

"Could your father or your brother have drawn them?" Tiffany asked.

Cradling her head in her hands, Audrey stared down at the contents of the folder. "My father was a farmer, first and foremost.

He never graduated from high school. All he ever did with a pencil was hand it to my mother. His world was his land, his animals, his crops, his family, and his faith. Period. And my brother, Larry, was all about math and numbers. He liked the things I drew, but that's where his interest ended."

Janet hummed in thought. "The plot thickens."

"It does, indeed," Audrey agreed. "Where did these drawings come from, and what are they doing in my mother's things?"

CHAPTER FOUR

Relishing the peace of Ranger's steady purring on her lap and Laddie's soft doggy snoring beside her, Janet drew in and released a deep breath. It had been a long day. Subtle aches surfaced in her arms and legs after all the lifting and squatting she'd done at the storage area that morning. And yet her mind spun.

Her husband divided his attention between the sitcom Tiffany had convinced them to try and the occasional chatter from the police scanner on the sofa table behind them.

"Ian?" Janet paused her hand—and thus the purring—atop Ranger's silky gray fur and waited for her husband's gaze to meet hers. "Do you ever wish you had a hobby of some sort?"

"What kind of hobby?" he asked.

"Like Harry enjoys watching the trains go by," Janet said as she once again stroked the cat's back.

Ian rubbed at the day's stubble on his chin. "Harry Franklin is ninety-six, Janet. He has time to sit at the station and watch the trains go by."

"Valid point." Janet cast about for another example, happily landing on one delivered to her proverbial doorstep in the past week. "Debbie says Greg likes going fishing with Jaxon and Julian."

"Fishing?" Ian repeated.

"That's right."

"One second." Ian leaned toward the hallway and called, "Tiff?"

"Yeah, Dad?"

"Any interest in going fishing with me this summer?"

"Not even a little bit!"

Janet resisted the urge to roll her eyes, and moved on. "Brendan is into working out, isn't he?" Several young women in town had their eye on the young deputy.

Ian's answering laugh drowned out Tiffany's approaching giggle. "Brendan is single. He's trying to win a Janet for himself. I've already got one."

"Wow. Nice one, Dad," Tiffany said.

"I thought so." Ian was waiting with a wink when Tiffany rounded the corner into the living room, and then he turned back to Janet. "Anyway, to answer your question, I'm not a hobby kind of guy, I guess."

"But hobbies can be a good release, especially for someone with a stressful career like yours."

Ian sobered. "I'm the police chief in Dennison, Ohio, Janet, not Columbus or Cleveland or Cincinnati. I have moments of stress, but they're not the norm. You know that."

"Hobbies bring joy and a sense of accomplishment."

Tiffany clapped a hand over her mouth, but her chuckle was still audible.

Ian squinted at Janet. "Is this about my birthday? Because if it is, I tell you what I want every single year."

Tiffany sent Janet a grin that clearly said *I told you so* over her father's head.

She scowled in reply. "Ian, I make you cookies and scones and cakes and pies all the time. I make them for you here at home, and I make them for you and the entire station on a weekly—if not more often—basis. I can't make that your birthday present too. It's not special enough."

"If it's what I want, why not?" he asked.

Ignoring Tiffany's smug smile, Janet searched every nook and cranny of her brain for something, anything, that might serve as a more celebratory option. "What about something for the garage? Like shelves for your tools?"

"Shelves for *Dad's* tools?" Tiffany snorted.

"Now, now, don't be so hard on your mom, Tiffany. I own a hammer. And I think there's a screwdriver in the junk drawer." They exchanged grins.

"Keep having fun at my expense. I don't mind." Janet addressed their pets. "Your dad and your sister are not being very nice to your mother right now. And all she's trying to do is make a nice birthday for one of them."

Leaning across the arm of his recliner, Ian captured Janet's hand in his own. "Seriously, Janet. Please don't make a big fuss. It's just another day. As long as you and Tiffany are part of it, I'll be happy."

"It's the day you came into the world, Ian. So, no, it's not 'just another day.' It's a special day. A day to celebrate you. To let you know how much you're loved and—"

A stream of steady beeps from the police scanner sent Ian scrambling for his phone. He skimmed the screen then slid his feet into his shoes and stood. "The first deputy on scene is fairly confident the report of a suspected break-in at the public works facility is a false alarm, but I probably should head out there to make sure. I'll do my best to get back as soon as possible."

"I understand." Janet pushed herself off the couch, much to the dismay of Ranger and Laddie, to hug and kiss her husband. "Be careful."

"Always." Ian made his way to the front door then paused. "I don't need a wrapped gift to know you love me, Janet. You show me that every day."

Then, with a wave at Tiffany, he yanked the door open and headed out into the dusk.

"Well, there you go."

Janet raised her eyebrows. "There I go, what?"

"Proof that you don't need to worry so much about what to get Dad for his birthday." Tiffany perched on the ottoman to put on her shoes. "Instead, you should worry about his reaction when he walks into a party he probably doesn't want either."

"Turning forty-five is a big deal," Janet protested. "Of course he's going to get a party."

Tiffany laughed. "Oh, I know he's getting one, but I'm not convinced he'll be all that thrilled about it. Dad isn't Mr. Center of Attention."

"On his birthday he can and should be." Janet sat down on the couch again, and Ranger and Laddie tucked themselves around her once more. "Just as he can, should, and *will* have a birthday present from his wife that isn't a baked good."

"Better watch out, Laddie." Tiffany leaned over and planted a kiss on the Yorkshire terrier's head. "Mom is showing her inner guard dog. Your job's in jeopardy."

Janet dropped her head back against the couch. "I want to do something special for your dad. He works so hard all the time."

Tiffany pivoted from the ottoman to the couch and took Janet's hand. "I think the party is a nice idea, Mom. I really do. I think Dad's gonna be embarrassed by all the attention, but I think he'll be glad you did it in the end. I also know you're gonna pull out all the stops." She squeezed Janet's fingers. "I'll be here when you need me."

"I'm counting on that, sweetheart."

"Good. It'll be fun decorating and helping you bake, plus keeping Dad in the dark about what's going on."

Janet slid her hand out from under Tiffany's and sat up. "But I can't give him *nothing*."

"I'm not suggesting you give him nothing, Mom. I'm suggesting you bake it, like he asked."

"Noted." Janet grinned as Ranger rolled onto his back, all four paws waving in the air. She reached out to rub his stomach and asked, "Do you know if there are any concerts coming up in Cleveland or Columbus that he might enjoy?"

"Not off the top of my head, but I'll look into it."

"Thank you." Janet appraised her daughter from head to toe and smiled. "What are you and Ashling up to this evening?" Ashling Kelly was Tiffany's close friend.

Tiffany stood and smoothed her hand down the front of the prairie-style top she'd paired with jeans. "We're going to a movie and then out for ice cream to catch up."

"Sounds fun. Be sure to give her my love and tell her to stop by the café one day soon so I can get a hug before she grows another foot."

"She's nineteen, Mom, like me. I'm pretty sure we're both done growing at this point." Tiffany gave Janet a peck on the forehead. "Love you, Mom. I'll be home by eleven."

Janet watched her daughter cross the room and pull open the same door Ian had walked through minutes earlier. "Be careful."

"I will."

And then Janet was alone. She shut off the TV and carefully—so as not to disturb Ranger or Laddie—plucked the latest installment in her favorite mystery series off the end table.

Several pages in, she realized she'd absorbed very little, if anything. Instead of jumping in with the beloved characters, she found herself thinking about the drawings they'd found and the animated short film on which they'd been based.

There was so much about the World War II era she found fascinating—veterans' stories of time spent in service and the trains filled with soldiers that had passed through Dennison. She relished the opportunities to talk to and befriend so many impacted by that time in history. But the icing on the cake was opening the café with Debbie in the same spot where so many soldiers had been fed between 1942 and 1946.

Janet had always felt she had a strong knowledge of that particular time period in American history. But after the information Tiffany had shared about the use of animation in the war effort, it was clear there was still a lot she didn't know.

A vibration from the end table pulled her from her thoughts. When she saw her daughter's name on her phone, she scooped it up at once.

"Tiffany?" she said, breathless with worry. "Are you okay?"

"I'm fine, Mom. I'm at the theater, waiting for Ashling to come out of the restroom. I just wanted to let you know that the movie is a long one and I probably won't be home until midnight."

A warm sensation started in the center of her chest and radiated out to her limbs. "I really appreciate you letting me know."

Tiffany laughed. "I didn't want you to wake up at two minutes after eleven and freak out because I'm not there."

Janet laughed along with her. "You know me so well. Now go have fun. I'm sitting here trying to read my book."

"Trying? It's no good?"

"I can't tell yet. My mind is too busy drifting."

"Dad's present again?"

"No, not this time. This time it's the stuff you told me this morning about animation and how it was used during the war."

"Cool, right?"

"Yeah. I'd like to learn more about it, quite frankly. Especially the short those drawings were based on."

"You should reach out to my professor, Joseph Carter. He loves to talk about the history of film."

"The school year is over, Tiffany. I'm quite sure he doesn't need the parent of one of his former students haranguing him about World War II short films during his break."

"Dr. Carter teaches at the school year-round because he loves what he teaches. He'll talk to anyone about it. Trust me on this," Tiffany said. "Anyway, Ashling is out, and we're going to head inside the theater now. I'll text you Dr. Carter's contact info so you can reach out to him if you want, and he can decide whether he wants to talk to you or not. Okay?"

How she loved having her daughter home. It made everything feel whole again. "Sounds good."

"Love you, Mom."

"Love you too, sweetheart."

CHAPTER FIVE

*E*arth to Janet. Come in, Janet."

Glancing up from the table she was wiping, Janet took in her friend's amused expression. "I'm here."

"Are you sure?" Debbie sat down in one of the chairs at the table and gestured for Janet to sit in another. "You've been wiping this table for close to a full minute. Same spot the whole time."

Janet stared at the table and then sat down. "I didn't realize. Sorry."

"No apologies. This table is the cleanest it's ever been," Debbie joked. Then she sobered. "You haven't been yourself all day. Everything okay?"

"Yeah, I'm fine. Typical Tuesday." Janet switched the placement of the tabletop salt-and-pepper shakers then switched them back.

Debbie plucked the shakers from her hands. "Something is clearly weighing on you, Janet. Spill."

Dropping her hands into her lap, Janet exhaled a long, deep breath. "Not weighing. Just distracting, I guess. It's about Ian."

Debbie leaned forward, concern etching fine lines in her forehead. "Is he sick?"

"No," Janet reassured her immediately. "It's nothing like that."

"Then what is it?"

"I'm just obsessing—that's all."

"About?"

"Ian's party."

"What about it?"

Janet buried her face in her hands. "Everything. What colors to use for the decorations. Whether any of our friends will slip up and blow the surprise. What music, if any, we should play. Whether the food I'm planning will be enough or too much. If he's going to get upset with me for throwing him a surprise party. What I can possibly get him that he'll actually like. I could continue, because I'm always thinking of new things to worry about. Tiffany thinks I'm crazy, and I'm beginning to wonder about that myself."

"I wouldn't say crazy." Debbie reached across the table and took Janet's hand. "Worrying needlessly, maybe. Ian's party will be wonderful, and you'll have all the help you need for it. Whatever colors you pick will be great. His friends know it's a surprise and will keep it that way. Whatever music you go with will merely be a backdrop to the many conversations. The food part is a nonissue with you at the helm. No matter how Ian feels initially, he'll know the party came from a place of love—from the woman he loves. And as far as a present goes, it'll come to you. So no worries, okay? The finish on this table can't take it."

Her friend was right. She was borrowing trouble where none existed.

Resting her chin on her hand, Janet smiled at Debbie. "Not sure what I did to have God put you in my life, but I'm grateful. To Him and to you."

"The feeling is mutual, my friend." Debbie glanced around the café but made no move to stand. "Ecstatic about having Tiffany back home?"

At the mere mention of her daughter, Janet felt the rest of her party-related tension evaporate. "I can't even begin to tell you how much I love it. Ian does too. I mean, we found our stride with her being off at school, but having her home just feels right. Listening to her and Ian tease each other, watching her play with the pets, having her walk into the kitchen and start chattering away about this, that, or the other—it's the best."

"Think she'd want to work here this summer?" Debbie asked. "Or is she going to lifeguard again?"

"I think she might enjoy filling in once in a while, if her schedule allows it. At least I hope so anyway. I'm anxious to soak up every minute I can with her in whatever way I can. You and I both know the summer will fly by, as it always does. We'll be dropping her off at Case Western for another year away before we know it."

"You two will make time for each other regardless of what job she gets. I'm sure of that." Debbie pushed her chair back. "Like you did yesterday."

"Ah, yes. Quality time going through boxes in a ten-by-ten windowless room." Janet laughed.

"Absolutely. I saw your smiles when you came in here afterward. It was obvious you enjoyed each other's company."

Janet smiled at the memory of the day. "I loved everything about Tiffany being little. Playing dolls or dress-up, reading books to her, everything. But seeing her become an adult is pretty spectacular too. In fact, thanks to a mysterious set of drawings we ran across yesterday, I learned something about World War II that I never knew before."

Debbie's eyes brightened. "Mysterious how?"

"We don't know who drew them or why they were in with Audrey's mother's things," Janet said. "Audrey doesn't know anything about them."

"Interesting," Debbie mused. "Why do you think her mother didn't draw them? Isn't that the most logical answer?"

"Audrey is adamant that's not possible," Janet said. "And now I want to learn more about the use of animation in the war effort."

"That shouldn't be too hard to do considering where we live and the wealth of information at our fingertips thanks to Kim and Eileen."

Janet stood as a group of customers came through the front door. "Don't forget Harry and Ray. They're all on my list to talk to the next time I see them." Her phone vibrated in her apron pocket, and she took it out and read the screen. "Cleveland?" she murmured. "I don't know anyone in—"

She gasped and grabbed Debbie's arm. "I think this is Tiffany's professor about the drawings."

Debbie waved Janet away. "Shoo. The display case is full, and Paulette will be here soon."

"Thanks." Janet headed out into the depot's large lobby area and hit the green button on her phone. "Hello? This is Janet Shaw."

"Mrs. Shaw, hello. This is Joseph Carter from Case Western. I received your email this morning. Is this a good time for us to talk?"

"Dr. Carter, yes. Thank you for calling. I'm sorry to bother you after you've just finished up the semester."

"Did a semester end?" He chuckled. "I've been told I'm a bit of a workaholic. Considering that I have a daybed in my office, that's probably a fair assessment."

She liked this man and his light spirit. "Whatever you're doing, you must be doing it right. My daughter, Tiffany, raves about your class. She went into it to get an elective out of the way and ended up loving it."

Another rich laugh. "That's music to my ears, Mrs. Shaw." He was quiet for a moment, and then he said, "In your email you said you are interested in learning about the use of animation during World War II?"

"Yes. Tiffany and I came across some drawings yesterday that she recognized from a short film shown during the war. She told me how animation was used to build public morale."

"That's true," Dr. Carter said. "Animated short films ran the gamut of subject matter, depending on the intended audience."

Janet settled onto one of the antique benches that filled the waiting area. "Tiffany mentioned that some of the films were made specifically for the soldiers."

"They were. It was an easy way to teach them the proper way to use and clean their weapons, how to identify the enemy, and what to do if they were captured. The animated short films shown at home were different. Some allowed people to release their anger and fear by ridiculing the enemy. Others were simply to provide entertainment centered around the war or to encourage doing one's part."

"The drawings we found were definitely based on a short that fell into the latter camp."

"Do you know which film?" he asked.

Janet thought for a moment. "If she told me the name of it, I don't remember. But it showed a young woman picking strawberries in a field and putting them in buckets. A little boy, watching her from between the slats of a fence, is rewarded at the end with a strawberry."

"Ah yes, I know the one you mean," Dr. Carter said. "The animator was Kenneth Hartman. It was called *Need It? Grow It.* And it showed how women in the heartland were helping offset food shortages by growing fruits and vegetables and sharing them with others in their communities. It was quite a departure from Hartman's other work at that time, but it was also the one that led to his immense success after the war."

Janet made a mental note of that information. "I don't know if you're aware, but Tiffany is from Dennison, a town that's rich in World War II history."

"I do remember that. She mentioned it early on, and I remember wishing I had time to pick her brain about the area, especially when she said her mother owns a café in the same depot that held the famous Dreamsville, USA, canteen." Interest filled his voice. "Tell me about that, if you would."

"As you probably know, our train depot saw lots of soldiers come through on their way to war. It provided a break in their journeys, where soldiers could step off the train to get some air and stretch their legs. Nearly four thousand volunteers set up and ran the canteen here from March 1942 to April 1946, supporting the service members and the war effort as a whole. They provided good food, reading materials, a place to socialize, and the assurance that the men and women had the support of their nation."

"I can't imagine how that must have felt for them."

"Long after the war, trains continued to come through our depot until the last passenger train in 1968 and, some twenty years later, the last freight train. Because of its rich history during the war era, the depot was restored. It now contains a museum and the Whistle Stop Café, which I co-own with my friend, Debbie Albright."

"Is the museum worth a trip down there?" he asked.

"It most certainly is. Kim Smith, the curator, has items on display that have been donated from families of World War II veterans. Purple Heart medals, uniforms, copies of recipes used to feed soldiers at the canteen, and so much more. Kim is the daughter of Eileen Palmer, the woman who was stationmaster during the war. Eileen still lives in the area, and the uniform she wore for her role as stationmaster is on display. The museum also has many interactive displays—great for adults and kids alike."

"It sounds wonderful," he said.

"Kim has an extensive collection of World War II-era records that she plays in the background most days. The best part of this town, though, is that in addition to Eileen Palmer, we still have a few other living residents who served." Janet glanced up at the Whistle Stop Café ribbon-cutting photo. The matching smiles she and Debbie wore, surrounded by so many special people, ignited a fresh delight she felt clear down to her toes. "And getting to spend time with them at the occasional town festival is a tremendous honor for anyone who will listen."

"If only more people felt the same. Because, before we know it, they'll be gone."

She didn't need a mirror to know her smile had faded in the wake of Dr. Carter's words—words she knew were true yet couldn't make herself embrace. "I understand, from my daughter, that you have quite a collection of animated films from that time."

"I do."

"I'd love to see them. If you ever find yourself with time on your hands, perhaps you could do a program about them here in Dennison? I'm quite sure others would be as intrigued by them as Tiffany and I are."

"I'd be honored," he said. "Very much so, in fact. But for now, I'd be happy to set aside a little time to show you my collection if you're ever in this area. Under one condition, if I may."

She grinned. "Tiffany told you about my scones, didn't she?"

"Your scones?"

At the confusion in his voice, she felt her cheeks grow warm. "I'm sorry. I assumed Tiffany was touting my blueberry scones the way she's done most of her life."

"I like scones."

She laughed. "I'll keep that in mind."

"I'd appreciate that. But no, my condition—which isn't really a true condition—is about the drawings you mentioned, the ones fashioned after Kenneth Hartman's short. Are they any good?"

"They're amazing. When Tiffany flipped through them in the way she said it would have been done during filming, I could actually picture sitting in a movie theater during the war, watching it on the screen."

"I'd love to see them if you think you'll find yourself up in Cleveland anytime soon."

"I'll have to ask their owner if I can borrow them."

"Do you think it would be a problem?"

"I can't imagine it would. Especially since she didn't even realize she had them until yesterday. But I do still need to ask." Janet lowered her phone to reference her digital calendar. Her week gave her a single option to meet with the professor, and it was short notice. Still, she threw it out. "I'm leaving work a little early tomorrow for an appointment. If all goes according to plan, I could be in Cleveland around six, if that would work for you."

"That's great for me. I'll have my collection of shorts cued and ready to go," he said with obvious excitement.

"Perfect." She made a mental note to reach out to Audrey about the drawings. "How do I find you on campus?"

"My office is on the second floor of the Mather House. Room 215."

She committed the information to memory and reached for the café door. "Thank you, Dr. Carter. I look forward to it."

CHAPTER SIX

*E*ven now, twenty-plus years after she'd graduated from Cleveland State University, Janet felt a familiar pull of excitement as she stepped onto the campus that was her daughter's new home-away-from-home during the school year. Like many college campuses, buildings rose between lush trees and sidewalks wound from one to the other. Large green spaces, perfect for outdoor study sessions on a blanket, flanked her on both sides. She lifted her face to the noon sun, reveling in the warmth it provided.

Student traffic was light on that Wednesday summer evening—a young man with a backpack coming down the sidewalk toward her, a pair of young women sitting opposite each other at a picnic table with remnants of a take-out order between them, and a prospective student soaking up everything a student tour guide said while her parents walked, hand in hand, a few steps behind. Even before the summer term officially started, a crackle of excitement hovered in the air, and Janet was happy to breathe it in. She wished Tiffany were there with her, but she had already made plans with her friends.

Janet glanced down at the map Tiffany had printed for her from the university's website and then headed toward the history building, the rapid and steady click of her heeled sandals an audible giveaway to the excitement she felt. The folder of pictures tucked safely under her left arm didn't belong to her, and their origins didn't impact her directly. But Tiffany's excitement and Audrey's confusion about them had raised her curiosity to a level she knew she had to address. For her own sake as much as anything else.

At the base of the building's steps, Janet drew in a breath and then quickly ascended to the glass doors at the top. She stepped inside, located the elevator, and rode it to the second floor.

She stepped out and found herself walking lightly so as not to intrude on the silence that felt sacred in the building. A directory placard on the wall led her down the hallway to her left, the sudden appearance of muting carpet a relief as she read the office numbers posted on each door.

She stopped outside the open door of Room 215, her gaze settling on a bearded man poring over an open book on his cluttered desk. Behind him, books filled every square inch of the built-in shelves that lined the back wall. To his right stood a gooseneck lamp clearly positioned to provide as much additional reading light as possible. To his left was a pair of cozy-looking chairs, angled so as to invite conversation between him and any coworkers or students who might stop by during the office hours posted on the door.

She knocked quietly on the door's trim. "Excuse me. Dr. Carter?"

He smiled broadly at her and pushed back his chair to stand. "Mrs. Shaw, I presume?"

"You presume correctly. But please call me Janet."

In several long strides, he was around his desk and greeting her at the door with an outstretched hand. "Janet it is. I'm Joe."

"It's nice to meet you. These are for you." She offered him a small white bakery bag.

His thick eyebrows furrowed for a moment before lifting as he peeked inside. "You brought the scones."

"I did."

He waved her inside and led her to the pair of chairs. "Please sit. Would you like a cup of coffee or a glass of water to go with your scone?"

"Thank you, but they're both for you. One blueberry, one raspberry."

"You won't join me?" he asked.

"I'd love a cup of coffee." She took the chair he indicated and watched as he crossed to a small coffee maker in one corner of the room. "I really appreciate your taking the time to see me, Joe."

He poured two mugs of coffee, added sugar and cream at her nod, and then settled in the chair opposite her. "I can't deny my interest in these drawings you mentioned on the phone yesterday afternoon. Is that them?" He nodded to the folder under her arm.

She set her coffee down on a small end table and moved the folder to her lap. "It is."

"And where did you come across these again?"

"They were in a storage facility. Tiffany was hired to go through the unit for a woman named Audrey Barker, who is new to Dennison. We found them in a box containing personal effects from Audrey's late mother."

Joe took a sip of his coffee. "Was the woman an artist?"

"The mother? No. Audrey is adamant about that," Janet replied. "But Audrey herself has talent."

"Any chance *she* drew them?" he asked.

"No. And it was quite clear that she'd never seen them before." Janet shrugged. "Sadly, as was often the case with the generation that raised her, she was taught to view art as something frivolous."

"Let me guess—Audrey became a teacher?"

"A nurse, actually," Janet said.

"A nurse," he repeated before setting down his cup. "The Greatest Generation did a lot right. They were the epitome of courage and displayed an admirable work ethic. But necessity was the name of the game in work and life, and they tended to instill that in their children as well."

Janet recalled the day she'd first met Audrey and the sketch that had stopped her in her tracks. "That's true. But when you see a talent like Audrey's and know in your heart it could have taken her somewhere with the right support, it's hard not to feel disappointed for her."

"How old is this woman? It's never too late to pursue a talent," Joe said.

She smiled. "She's seventy-one. And Tiffany told her the same thing. You're both right. But Audrey doesn't feel that way."

Joe leaned forward. "May I see the drawings?"

"Of course." Janet held the folder out to him and watched as he set it on his lap and eagerly flipped open the cover.

A long, low whistle escaped his lips as he stared down at the first drawing. Even from her vantage point, Janet found herself marveling all over again at the exquisite detail—the sun glinting off the farmhouse roof in the distance, the plump strawberries peeking out from rows and rows of green leaves, and the sturdy white fence that bordered the plentiful crop on the left.

"This is incredible." He flipped to the next picture and pointed out the inclusion of an empty bucket and a pair of dusty bare feet visible beneath it.

He flipped to the next, and the next, and the next. The story of the woman and the neighborhood boy played out with each new drawing.

"These are spot-on to Hartman's work. The colors, the facial expressions, the detail, everything," he murmured as he reached the final drawing. "Spot-on."

"Tiffany said as much."

Again, he took in the drawings, slowly flipping his way through each one from back to front, and front to back. "And these were in a box?"

"They were."

"In order?" he asked.

"No. Tiffany ordered them based on her memory."

He smiled. "She clearly paid attention. She got it exactly right."

"She loved your class." Janet took another sip of her coffee. "Especially the section about animated short films. She said these drawings were fashioned after her favorite one of all."

"They're amazing," he mused, his voice suddenly husky. "The detail. The accuracy. These appear to have been drawn frame by frame, or rather cel by cel. Clearly, whoever made these drawings felt a deep connection to this film." He studied the first few again and then met Janet's gaze. "This particular animated short has always fascinated me. Not because of its subject matter but because of how different it was."

"But from what you said on the phone yesterday, it sounded like there were other animated shorts like this one," Janet said, frowning.

"There were. Many, in fact. But I'm talking about the difference for Kenneth Hartman. The rest of his work during that time was aimed toward the soldiers. It was darker, harsher. Whereas this"—he tapped the first drawing—"is lighter, more hopeful. The colors, the backdrop, the child, all of it."

Janet considered the professor's words. "Maybe he wanted to try something different after the heaviness of his other work."

Joe thumbed through the pictures again and then closed the folder and handed it back to her. "Maybe. It's *very* different, as you're about to see."

She smiled. "You're going to show me some of the shorts from your collection?"

"That was our deal, wasn't it?" he asked. "Let me grab the television cart from the AV room. You're in for a real treat."

CHAPTER SEVEN

*J*anet had zero regrets over her decision to partner with Debbie to open and run the Whistle Stop Café. The chance to bake her mornings away, to watch friends and strangers enjoying her efforts, to provide a gathering place in a historically rich location, and to do all those things alongside her best friend had proven to be everything she'd hoped and so much more.

Yet, on Thursday afternoon, she couldn't deny the relief she felt as she left the café after another successful day. It wasn't that she was tired of being a floured mess or that she was especially anxious to give her mouth a break from talking. It was, rather, about finally being free to visit the museum and pick the director's brain.

She listened to the quiet murmurings on the other side of the depot. Unlike the café, where conversation and laughter flowed at a variety of volumes, the museum seemed to have an unspoken rule that yielded more whispering and softened exclamations. At least on days no school bus was parked out front.

Tugging the strap of her tote bag onto her shoulder, Janet crossed the tiled floor and stepped inside the open museum doorway, admiring the life-size photograph of Eileen Palmer during her days as wartime stationmaster and the mannequin shape beside it that wore her uniform. Nearby was the glass case that housed a rotating display of World War II artifacts. She found Kim standing by in case the trio of guests perusing the room had any questions. As Janet stepped closer, Kim turned her way, her smile widening.

"Hi, Janet," she said. "Quitting time for you already?"

"That's right," Janet said. "Busy day here too?"

The sparkle in Kim's eye gave Janet her answer loud and clear. Before the curator could speak, one member of the trio deposited a ten-dollar bill in the donation case, thanked Kim, and then hurried to catch up with the rest of his group as they left.

"Busy *and* great," Kim said to Janet. "Lots of really interesting people visited today, including the son of a soldier, who came here because he wanted to see the place his father had mentioned in a letter during the war."

"That's fantastic."

"Wait. It gets better." Kim disappeared behind the counter and returned with a piece of yellowed, tri-folded paper and an equally yellowed envelope. "He offered to leave his father's letter with me for next month's mini exhibit—one I'd already decided to call 'Letters From War.'"

"Wow. What are the odds of that?"

Kim ran her fingers carefully over the envelope. "Dennison and the canteen are not only mentioned. They're praised to the heavens for the support they offered. It makes his father's letter even more perfect for the exhibit."

When Kim talked about such things, Janet was always struck by her friend's heartfelt passion for history—a passion that had been aroused in Janet herself thanks to her visit with Tiffany's college professor the previous evening.

"Have you ever considered doing a display about the use of animation during the war?" Janet asked.

Kim carefully set the envelope and letter on top of the counter. "I hadn't, but I'm all ears."

"As you probably know, animated short films were used to teach soldiers about battle and the enemy, and they were also used to encourage support for the war effort here on the home front. Tiffany took a history elective this past semester, and she learned about these animated shorts. Her teacher has an extensive collection of them, and they're quite fascinating."

"I was aware of those films, but it's not an area I've researched much. Though I did read something about it recently." Kim tapped her finger on her chin. "But where I read about it, or in what publication, I don't have the foggiest clue. Maybe in a newspaper or something I came across online?"

After a minute, Janet said, "Anyway, if you think you'd be interested in seeing the collection of animated short films I mentioned—"

Kim held up one hand. "I'm sorry, but can you hold that thought for a second? I think I remember what I read about animation the other day."

She hurried around the counter and opened her laptop.

Seconds later, Kim began to read aloud. "'The family of the late Kenneth Hartman, a well-known animator, is opening his vast vault of material for an exhibit that will tour several major cities this fall. This opportunity will allow attendees to get up close and personal with the animator's countless career highlights. It will also provide a behind-the-scenes look at the objects and people that served as inspiration for some of his beloved work, both during and after World War II."

"Kenneth Hartman?" Janet echoed. "Seriously?" What were the odds?

"That's right. The exhibit will kick off in Seattle. It'll move on to Dallas and DC and then culminate with a slightly longer run in New York City."

"Where did you find that?"

"In the *Pittsburgh Post-Gazette*."

Janet rounded the counter to join Kim at the computer and silently read the remainder of the article. When she reached the bottom line, she sucked in a breath. "His granddaughter lives a little over an hour from here, in a suburb west of Pittsburgh."

"Small world, right?"

"I'd love to talk to her. Especially after finding Audrey's pictures and getting to watch the short they were based on with Tiffany's professor the other day. Will you send this article to me?"

Kim did so then shut the laptop. "You should reach out to her."

"The granddaughter?" Janet asked. "Do you really think I should?"

"Why not? What can it hurt?" Kim grabbed a dustcloth from a drawer behind the counter and made her way to a display case. "In my experience, people love to talk about their loved ones' contributions to the war. As they should, I might add."

"I suppose," Janet hedged.

Kim crossed to the case near her mother's display and pointed to a series of war medals alongside a collection of artifacts. "A visitor told me about the veteran who owned these a few months ago. She gave me a contact number for the veteran's daughter, and I reached out to her. She was positively over the moon to have someone show interest in her dad. And when I asked if she'd consider sharing some of his medals and canteen memorabilia for a temporary exhibit here, she was so happy she cried, knowing that her father's sacrifice would be seen and recognized by a whole new generation of people. That's been my experience more often than not."

It made sense. It really did. But—

"You can't get a yes if you don't ask, right?" Kim prodded.

Janet pulled her friend in for a quick hug. "You're right, Kim, I can't."

CHAPTER EIGHT

Holding perfectly still as directed, Janet smiled at the little girl with a single carnation bloom in one hand and a pin in the other.

"Happy Mother's Day, Mrs. Shaw." The child carefully pinned the flower in place.

"Thank you, Cynthia." Janet breathed in the faint floral scent then hugged the second grader. "What a very nice thing for your Sunday school class to do for all us women today. You're making us feel very special, that's for sure."

A rare burst of shyness yielded her a whispered "You're welcome" in return before the child moved on to the next woman entering the fellowship hall after the morning service.

Straightening to her full height, Janet smiled at her daughter. "You weren't much older than that when you gave me this necklace for Mother's Day." She lifted the silver heart-shaped pendant at her throat for Tiffany to see. "Yet, here you are, home from your first year at college, and I have absolutely no idea how it happened."

Ian stepped up beside Janet and wrapped his arm around her shoulders. "We blinked, that's how. She did it when our eyes were closed."

"Hello? I'm still here." Tiffany spread her arms wide. "Still cute. Still fun. Still me. See?"

"You are pretty cute. Most of the time," Ian teased.

"Dad!"

Janet reveled in the joy of being with two of her greatest blessings and kissed them both on the cheek. "If we don't get a move on, there'll be no doughnuts left for the two of you. And I have it on good authority there are cider ones today."

Ian pivoted so quickly he nearly knocked Debbie over. "I'm sorry, Debbie." He made sure she was steady on her feet then looked at Tiffany and hooked his thumb at the folding table along the back wall. "Race you."

"Sometimes I still pinch myself when I look at them," she said to Debbie as her husband and daughter reached their intended destination and celebrated their victory by pumping the air with their fists.

"Of course you do. They're the best." Debbie pulled Janet in for a heartfelt hug. "Happy Mother's Day, my friend."

"Thanks, Debbie." She sized up her longtime pal. "Why, Debbie, you're beautiful. That color is stunning on you."

Something about the sudden flushing of her friend's cheeks sent Janet's gaze following after Debbie's to…*Greg*. And he was gazing right back at Debbie.

"Happy Mother's Day, Janet."

Startled, Janet swung her attention away from Debbie to an increasingly familiar face. "Audrey, you made it! Did you enjoy the service?"

Audrey scanned the room. "I did. Very much."

"I'm sorry I didn't see you come in. I would have loved for you to sit with me and my family."

"That's okay," Audrey said. "Two people invited me to sit with them when it became clear I was by myself. So we all sat together."

Janet beamed. "I'm happy to hear that. And I'm happy you stayed for doughnuts. It's an annual tradition following the service on Mother's Day. In addition, every woman gets a carnation corsage from the second-grade Sunday school class."

Audrey patted the carnation pinned to her blouse. "It's really a nice tradition."

At the subtle rasp in the woman's answer, Janet stepped closer. "I'm sure you're missing your mother even more than usual today. How are you holding up?"

Audrey gave up on her weak attempt at a smile and shrugged. "I expected last year's Mother's Day to be hard—and it was. I cried off and on most of the day. I thought I'd be okay a whole year later." She tried to blink away the tears filling her eyes. "But it's still hard."

"I'm sorry." Janet meant it. She couldn't imagine not having her own mother around to celebrate on this day.

Audrey drew in a breath, squared her shoulders, and motioned at the people around them. "But I'm here, people have been kind, and when I get home, I'm going to make a cup of hot cocoa even though it's seventy degrees out, because that's something Mama and I liked to do together after church. Then, after that, I'm going to sit down and go through some of her personal things. That way, it might feel like we're spending part of Mother's Day together."

Janet took Audrey's hand in hers and gently squeezed. "I think that sounds like a lovely idea, Audrey."

"We got there in time," Ian announced, reclaiming his spot beside Janet with a half-eaten doughnut in one hand and an untouched doughnut on a napkin in the other. "Happy Mother's Day, my love." He caught sight of Audrey. "Oh, I'm sorry. I didn't mean to interrupt." He shifted his doughnut onto the napkin beside Janet's, dusted his hand on his pants, and then offered it to Audrey. "I'm Ian Shaw. Janet's husband."

"Hi, Ian." Audrey slipped her hand from Janet's gentle grasp and returned Ian's handshake. "I'm Audrey Barker. Your wife was kind enough to invite me to visit your church today."

"Then you get this, if it's all right with the original recipient." At Janet's nod, Ian handed the uneaten doughnut to Audrey. "You're the woman who hired our daughter to go through your storage unit."

"I am."

"Are you getting settled in your new home?" he asked.

"It's coming along. Slowly but surely."

"I'm glad to hear that," Ian said. "Not only is Dennison a nice place with nice people, it also has really good desserts. Many made, coincidentally, by my wife."

Janet held her palms against her warming cheeks. "My husband is a little biased, I'm afraid."

"I wouldn't call him biased," Audrey told her. "Not after eating your chocolate cream pie."

"Told you so." Ian gave Janet a smug smile then excused himself to speak with one of his officers.

"Ian is the chief of the Dennison Police Department," Janet explained to Audrey. "In much the way small-town teachers seem to know everyone, so does he."

Audrey took a bite of the doughnut and hummed with delight. "And he's clearly a good judge of treats."

Janet stepped closer to Audrey and lowered her voice. "I'm throwing Ian a surprise party on his birthday, which is the last day of the month. The party itself will come together fine, I'm sure. At least I'm hoping it will. But the gift part? He refuses to give me any ideas or hints. He keeps asking me to bake him something, which I do all the time. It's infuriating."

"Does he have any hobbies?" Audrey asked.

"No."

"Does he need anything for work?"

"I tried that. No luck."

Audrey finished her doughnut and wiped her hands with the napkin. "I picked up an accent in Ian's voice. Is he Scottish?"

"That's right," Janet said. "He was born there and came to the States with his parents at a young age."

"What about a gift having to do with Scotland?"

"I themed a small family party around Scotland for him five or six years ago. I tracked down a map of the country based on family clans and a small jar filled with Scottish soil for him. He thanked me, but last I saw, both items are still in their original boxes in his closet." Janet sighed. "The part he liked best about the party was the Scottish tablet and the *cranachan* I made for it. Those are Scottish desserts, and I found traditional recipes for them. Tablet is basically crystallized sugar and cream, served in squares that melt in your mouth. Cranachan is a layered dessert like trifle, with cream, raspberries, and oats. I think Ian ate half of each by himself."

Audrey laughed. "So desserts really *are* his thing."

"Desserts and my mom." Tiffany appeared beside Janet and exchanged hellos with Audrey. "Which, if you think about it, is pretty awesome."

"Agreed," Audrey said.

"You'll come, right?" Janet asked.

"Come to what?"

Janet lowered her voice still further. "To Ian's surprise party. It'll be at seven o'clock at the Whistle Stop two weeks from this coming Friday."

"You barely know me," Audrey protested. "And I met your husband less than five minutes ago."

Janet was already shaking her head before Audrey finished. "That doesn't matter. We have a good feeling about you. And it'll be a great way for you to get to know your Dennison neighbors."

"I don't know what to say," Audrey said, her voice soft yet pleased.

"Say you'll come," Tiffany urged.

"My daughter is right. Please say you'll come."

"Two weeks from Friday?" Audrey asked.

"Yes. May thirty-first at seven o'clock. Don't worry about bringing anything but yourself."

Audrey smiled. "I'll be there."

CHAPTER NINE

$\mathcal{J}$anet didn't need to see the near-empty scone, doughnut, and muffin display trays to know it had been a busy Monday morning at the café. That realization had become crystal clear when she'd watched the hours fly by on the kitchen clock and found herself unable to glance into the dining area, let alone take a break.

But it was a good problem to have.

In a matter of months, the business she and Debbie had taken a leap of faith to open had become a go-to spot for residents of Dennison and the surrounding towns. For regulars like Harry Franklin and his dog, Crosby, it was the perfect place to get a good breakfast and meet old and new friends. For others, like Harry's granddaughter, Patricia, it was perfect for grabbing coffee and a muffin on the way to work. Business meetings were often conducted over sandwiches and chips, while the next table was inhabited by a group of friends catching up over soup and salad or a piece of cake or pie.

Some of the appeal was based on the depot's convenient location. But Janet liked to think that a lot of it was the café itself. The pale yellow walls with deep red wainscoting, the white tin ceiling, and the abundance of natural light streaming through the large windows gave the dining area a warm and cozy feel while the ample tables and counter seating invited customers to stay a while.

Still, as wonderful as their success was, Janet was relieved that their morning had finally settled down. Checking the clock, she lifted her arms into the air in preparation for a much-needed stretch but paused as the kitchen door opened.

"Wow," Debbie said, stepping into the room. "You're still standing."

Janet finished her stretch. "I'm as surprised as you are."

"I'd have to check our records to be sure, but I'm pretty certain this was our busiest Monday morning to date. Paulette, who's been running all morning, agrees." Debbie eyed the pans and mixing bowls waiting for their chance at the dishwasher. "Returning customers were sharing their favorite breakfast items with newbies in line throughout the morning rush, and at least a dozen times someone who came in for something for themselves ended up getting a few extra for coworkers or a friend."

Janet jutted her chin toward the trash can in the corner. "That wouldn't have happened with the yogurt scones I destroyed."

Debbie peeked inside. "What happened?"

"The end result was supposed to come out fluffy and soft, but mine were flat as a board."

"That's okay. You'll figure it out. You always do." Debbie pulled a spoon from a nearby drawer and helped herself to some batter left on the edge of the mixing bowl used for blueberry muffins. "Are we good for the lunch crowd?"

Janet gestured at the cupcakes and brownies she'd made at five that morning. "We should be."

"Those look delicious," Debbie said. "Anyway, seeing as how the breakfast rush is nearly over, why don't you grab yourself some coffee and take a break? Paulette and I can handle things for a while.

The little table in the front corner is open, and you should be able to clear your head before we move into the lunch rush."

Janet tugged off her apron. "I'd like to say I don't need that, but—oh no, my necklace!" She reached down and scooped up the silver heart pendant from where it had fallen on the floor.

"What happened?" Debbie asked.

Janet examined the chain. "The clasp broke."

"That's easily fixed. The next time you're in New Philly, you can take it to the jeweler in that strip mall."

"Tiffany gave me this for Mother's Day years ago," Janet said.

"I remember. It's due for a little TLC." Debbie dropped the spoon into the sink and read Janet's pale green T-shirt. "'Bake the World a Different Place,' huh? I like it."

"I found it on a T-shirt site online and couldn't resist," Janet said, slipping the necklace into her purse.

"I'm glad you didn't. It suits you perfectly, since that's what you do every single day."

"We're closed on Sundays, remember?"

"Like that stops you from cooking and baking. Take your break." Debbie nudged Janet toward the coffee maker and the clean mugs positioned on an open shelf above it.

"Yes, ma'am." Janet grabbed a mug and filled it with coffee. "It looked like you and Greg were having a good talk after church yesterday. I saw you when Ian, Tiffany, and I were heading out."

Debbie grabbed a broom resting against the wall. "We were talking, sure. Nothing important though, as evidenced by the fact that I can't remember what we said."

"But you're enjoying each other, right?" Janet prodded.

"Yes. And how was your conversation with Audrey?"

"Audrey?"

"Yes. I saw you two talking after church as well."

Janet opened her mouth to challenge Debbie's clear redirection then chose to let it go. She pushed the swinging door open. "Audrey is a very nice woman. Lovely, in fact. Anyway, I'll take ten or fifteen minutes for my break, but let me know if you need me sooner."

"I will."

The door swung closed behind her, and Janet glanced around at the handful of customers seated around the room. A young man in a neon-yellow vest used his last bite of toast to sop up the rest of the egg on his plate. A group of four college-age boys talked and laughed across their empty plates and glasses at a corner table. At a window table, she recognized a familiar figure nursing what she knew was a mug of peppermint mocha.

The part of Janet that had been on her feet since five a.m. wanted to pass quietly on her way to the vacant corner table. But the part of her that loved Dennison and its close-knit community refused.

Holding her coffee mug steady, Janet crossed to the window. "Happy Monday, Patricia."

Patricia Franklin smiled up at Janet. "The apple cinnamon pastry was amazing, Janet."

"I'm glad." Janet nodded toward the stack of papers beside the attorney's empty plate. "Hard at work on a case?"

Patricia set her mug down. "I am. But nothing terribly fun, I'm afraid. Which is why I'm going over the file here instead of in my office. If the work isn't pleasant, at least my environment can be."

"Makes sense to me."

Janet gestured to the other customers. "I don't see your grandfather and Crosby. Are they okay?"

"They were on their way out when I arrived a little while ago. Pop Pop said Crosby has a checkup at the vet today."

"Ah, okay. Just a routine thing, right?" Janet asked.

"Thankfully, yes."

"Phew." Crosby had given them all a minor scare with his health a couple months before, and Janet was grateful to learn he was still doing well.

"I couldn't say it better myself. But I should probably get going. Duty calls." Patricia set her mug in the center of her empty plate, gathered her papers into the beautiful leather case her beloved Pop Pop had given her for her birthday, and stood. "Have a great day, Janet."

"You too, Patricia."

Janet started to backtrack to the register with Patricia but stopped when Debbie emerged from the kitchen. Grateful, Janet continued the rest of the way to the corner table and fairly dropped onto one of its two empty chairs, content to say and do nothing for the next ten minutes or—

"Janet!"

Freezing with her mug in midair, Janet took in the museum director hurrying toward her table with a sheet of paper in one hand and some money in the other. "Kim? Why aren't you relaxing at home? Isn't it your day off?"

"Yes, and I'm out and about because it's my day off," Kim explained. "This is the day I do all the things I can't do when the museum is open. Like errands and appointments and stuff like that."

Janet lowered her mug to the table. "Yet you're here."

"One of your cookies-and-cream cupcakes, along with a soda, will make all of that so much easier," Kim said, lifting a ten-dollar bill into the air.

"The carrot to get you to do your chores."

"And a better-tasting one than its namesake." Kim set the piece of paper on the table. "Plus, I knew you'd want this."

Janet raised an eyebrow, her curiosity piqued despite the lingering fatigue she desperately needed to shake. "What is that?"

"It's Stacy's phone number."

"Stacy?" Janet echoed, before stealing a sip of her cooling coffee. "I don't think I know her. Is that the name of the woman Pastor Nick brought in from Canton to help with updating the church directory?"

"No. Her name is Linda Murdock, I believe."

Janet took another sip of her coffee. "Okay, then what is this Stacy's last name? That could help me place her."

"Hartman." Kim sat down across the table from her and pushed the page closer to Janet. "Stacy Hartman."

Janet frowned at the name on the paper and then slid her gaze down to the phone number she didn't recognize. "Isn't this an area code near Pittsburgh?"

"That's right."

"Then I really have no idea who this—" Janet stopped as something clicked in her brain. "Hartman? As in the granddaughter of Kenneth Hartman? The one who was interviewed for that article you read to me on Saturday?"

"One and the same."

"You spoke to her?"

Kim beamed proudly. "I did."

"But how did you get her number?"

"I'm the curator of a museum, Janet. Research is my middle name."

Janet stared down at the name and number. "I don't know what to say. Or what I'm supposed to do with this."

"I told her about you." With her elbow propped on the edge of the table, Kim rested her chin on her palm. "And about Ian."

Janet drew back. "You told her about Ian? Why?"

"I figured she'd be less worried about meeting with you if she knew your husband was a police chief."

"Meeting with me?" Janet echoed. "Are you serious?"

Kim laughed. "I am. Now, all you have to do is call her so the two of you can decide on a date and time that works for both of you."

Janet's thoughts traveled back to the animated short films Joe Carter had shown her in his office and the near perfect yet anonymous drawings found in a box belonging to Audrey Barker's late mother—drawings based on one of Kenneth Hartman's most famous wartime animations.

"I'm not a museum curator like you, Kim. And I didn't even know these animated short films existed until Tiffany told me about them," Janet said. "Do you think she would take the time to talk to me?"

Kim sat back in her chair and studied Janet. "You're interested in her grandfather's work, right?"

"I am," Janet confirmed.

"Stacy is proud of him," Kim explained. "Having someone show interest means something. That's why she would take the time to talk to you."

"There's going to be a traveling exhibit about his work starting next fall, right? Why shouldn't I wait for that?"

Kim shrugged. "You can if you want. And if you feel like traveling to DC or New York to see it. Plus, we don't know whether she'll be traveling with the exhibit, and she's the one you want to talk to. She lives a little over an hour away from where we're both sitting right now, and she's willing to meet you. That seems like a win-win to me."

"I guess you're right."

"It's been known to happen," Kim teased as she stood. "I've got an appointment about thirty minutes away, and there's a cupcake and a soda that'll make my drive to get to it so much more appealing."

"Tell Debbie it's on the house," Janet said.

"You don't have to do that."

"I want to. It's the least I can do after you gave me this." Janet held up the paper.

"It was my pleasure." Kim made her way to the display case.

For a moment, Janet lost herself in the ensuing interaction between Kim and Debbie, and seconds later, Debbie handed Kim a to-go cup and the white paper bag containing her beloved cookies-and-cream cupcake. She saw Kim hold out her money and then lower it when Janet called Debbie's name and waved off the payment. Kim thanked them then headed out of the café.

Janet examined the name and number on the paper in front of her. She knew her mounting excitement at the thought of speaking with Stacy Hartman was a little odd. She didn't teach a class in which Stacy's grandfather was featured like Joe Carter did. She wasn't a college student who took to the man's work like Tiffany had. And she wasn't the owner of the box that had held such detailed drawings of his most well-known and respected wartime contribution.

What she *was*, though, was the co-owner of a café housed in a historic depot that had played a major part in World War II. Like her daughter, she had found Kenneth Hartman's *Need It? Grow It* piece of wartime history intriguing. She had been there when a series of detailed drawings based on that same piece of animation history had been found in a box of personal effects. She had witnessed Audrey Barker's stunned surprise at learning they'd been found inside a box belonging to her late mother, a woman Audrey was confident couldn't, and wouldn't, have drawn them.

Drawing in a breath, Janet reached into the front pocket of her pants and pulled out her phone. She tapped in the number on the paper and connected the call.

One ring.

Two rings.

Three—

"Hello?"

"Hi. My name is Janet Shaw. I believe you spoke with my friend, Kim Smith. She's the curator of a World War II museum here in Dennison."

"Hi, Janet." Excitement rang in Stacy's tone. "I was hoping you'd call."

"Y-you were?" she stammered. "Why?"

"Because you want to know more about my grandfather, and talking about him to someone who wants to listen helps me feel a little closer to him."

She considered Stacy's answer against everything Kim had said. Her friend had been completely right. "I haven't seen much of his work, but it's fascinating. And yes, I'd very much like to learn more."

"Where are you again?" Stacy asked.

"Dennison, Ohio."

"That's right. I could meet you somewhere if you'd like, or you're certainly welcome to come here to my house. I'd be happy to show you some of the things I've been pulling out for an exhibit next fall."

"To your house?" Janet repeated, stunned.

"I don't see why not. You can see his drawings and his pencils and his awards, plus whatever else I can find between now and then."

"But you don't know me."

"I learned enough from Kim to feel comfortable having you here," Stacy said. "But if that makes you uneasy, we could meet somewhere."

"I'd love to come to your house and see everything from your grandfather's career that you're willing to share with me," Janet said. "Would you mind if I brought my daughter, Tiffany? She's completed her first year at Case Western Reserve, and she's actually the one who told me about your grandfather's work in the first place."

"Not at all. Please bring her," Stacy said, her enthusiasm evident. "I'm free at six thirty on Wednesday if that works for you and your daughter?"

The arrival of a customer sent Janet's attention to the wall clock behind the counter. In another twenty minutes, the next round of craziness would take them all the way to their two o'clock closing.

"It does indeed," she confirmed to Stacy.

"Then it's a date. I'll text you my address when we hang up."

"Thank you, Stacy. I look forward to it."

CHAPTER TEN

*J*anet double-checked the number on the mailbox against the one in the text message Stacy had sent. The drive to Findlay, just west of Pittsburgh, had taken longer than she'd hoped thanks to some traffic at the midway point, but they'd made it.

Monday's busyness at the café had continued into Tuesday and today. It was a good problem to have, but it also left little time to think about anything besides what was ready to go in the oven, what was currently in the oven, and what was due to come out of the oven.

The car ride, though, had been a forced break. For her and, she suspected, for her unexpected copilot.

She smiled at Debbie. "I know I hit you with this at the last minute, but thanks for making the drive with me. I really appreciate it."

Debbie balled up the wrapper from the take-out meal they'd secured en route and added it to the bag at her feet. "Are you kidding? As if I'd give up a chance to talk without the kind of interruptions we have at the café all the time. Trust me, this has been a nice change of pace."

"I'm glad." Janet tossed her keys into her purse, plucked the bakery box from the floor behind Debbie's seat, and motioned for her friend to join her on the quiet street.

On their left, a small park with a playground and a few benches filled a green space between two houses. Up ahead, the cul-de-sac hosted nearly a dozen elementary-school kids, riding bikes, creating sidewalk chalk art, and shrieking during a lively game of tag.

Janet led Debbie toward the simple yet attractive two-story home they'd driven for over an hour to reach.

Together, she and Debbie stepped onto a walkway flanked by purple, yellow, white, and pink hyacinths, and followed it to the maroon-colored door that sported a patriotic wreath with a hand-painted WELCOME sign at its center. Janet lifted her hand to knock, but the door swept open, revealing a diminutive blond woman in her mid to late thirties.

"Janet Shaw?"

"That's me."

Their hostess's dazzling smile faltered a smidge as her gaze landed on Debbie. "And who's this?"

"I'm Janet's friend, Debbie Albright."

"I hope you don't mind, but I asked Debbie to come along when my daughter was unable to make it at the last minute," Janet added.

"I don't mind one bit." Stretching out her hand, the woman shook Debbie's. "I'm Stacy Hartman. Please come in."

Inside, Janet handed the box to Stacy. "I didn't know what you'd like, so I brought you a few different desserts to try as well as a few options for your breakfast tomorrow morning."

"You didn't have to do that," Stacy said, taking the box from her.

"You won't be saying that after you try what's inside," Debbie told her, smiling. "Janet's baked goods are legendary."

Stacy lifted the box's lid and peeked inside, her eyes widening. "You brought me cupcakes?"

"One chocolate and one vanilla, in case you're not a fan of chocolate."

"I'm a huge fan of both chocolate and vanilla." Stacy inhaled deeply. "Is that an apple cinnamon muffin?"

"It is. And the other is banana."

"Thank you so much." Stacy clutched the box with a smile. "I was born with a sweet tooth."

"A character trait that pleases me to no end," Janet said.

"Happy to hear it." Stacy chuckled and led Janet and Debbie into a small living area with a couch, an armchair, and a TV on a narrow stand. She ushered them to the couch while she perched on the edge of the chair. "In most people's homes, this would be the office space, and the larger room at the back of the house would be the living room. But, as you can see, that's not what I did, and the reason I didn't will make sense to you soon."

Janet made herself comfortable. "I'm excited to hear whatever you want to tell us."

"Your friend from the museum told me about the depot where your café is located and how it was related to the war. Do you have anything on your menu tied to that era?" Stacy asked.

"We have a few things, actually," Janet said. "An egg salad we offer at lunch is a throwback to that time. The recipe was given to us by a customer from the St. Louis area who visited the depot this past fall. His mother worked in a factory during the war, and she'd often share egg salad sandwiches with her fellow coworkers on a Friday afternoon."

Debbie settled into her corner of the sofa. "We also have a classic doughnut recipe from that era. It's the one they used to make and serve to the service members at the canteen."

"We do, indeed." Janet splayed her hands. "And we can't forget our hearty World War II era tomato soup or our Salisbury steak."

"You work at this café together?" Stacy asked.

"We co-own it," Debbie said. "Janet handles most of the baking, and I handle most of the front-counter stuff, but there's a lot of overlap too."

"That's lovely." Resting her elbows on the armrests of her chair, Stacy tented her fingers. "I can't imagine what it must have been like to live during a world war. Constant worry about whether your loved ones were okay, not knowing what you'd wake up to on any given day, concern about whether there'd be enough food to feed your family—all of it. Yet everyone did their part."

"The Greatest Generation," Janet mused. "A label that truly fits."

"There's so much we can learn from them, but it won't be long before they're all gone," Stacy said.

"It's sad," Janet agreed. "But that's why it's important that we find ways to remember their sacrifices. Like we try to do with the descriptions we give beneath wartime dishes on our menu. Like Kim does with the museum and her joy of talking about that time period with everyone who walks through its doors. And like you are doing by agreeing to share your grandfather's work for a traveling exhibit that could reach hundreds of thousands of people."

A smile broke over Stacy's face. "Hundreds of thousands of people," she repeated in a whisper. "Can you imagine if it did?"

"I can. And what a tribute that will be."

Her smile beginning to tremble, Stacy lifted her hands to her cheeks. "My grandpa made my childhood positively magical in every way possible, and I miss him as much today as I did when he passed eighteen years ago."

Janet leaned forward. "Tell us about him. Please."

"He saw the world differently, so he handled it differently. When I was little and would get excited about something that no one else thought twice about, he wouldn't pat me on the head and say 'That's nice, Stacy,' the way the other adults did. He tried to see through my eyes. And he encouraged me all the time and with everything I showed even the tiniest bit of interest in."

"He sounds like he was a truly wonderful grandpa," Debbie said.

Stacy swallowed hard, nodding. "He was the best." She dropped her gaze to the floor. "I wish I'd had the same interest in him and his story then as I do now."

Janet traded glances with Debbie. "How old are you, if you don't mind me asking?"

"Thirty-five."

"And he passed eighteen years ago?"

"Yes."

"So you were seventeen." Janet scooted forward on the sofa. "You were a teenager."

"I was. But I still could have asked and listened more," Stacy said.

Janet patted Stacy's arm. "You clearly know enough to realize how interesting his work will be to so many. And you're honoring his memory."

"Because I finally asked and listened. But it wasn't him talking."

Janet sat back on the couch. "Your father?"

"I wish. He passed shortly after my grandfather. But my mom told me as much as she could. The rest of what I've come to know about Grandpa Ken came from things left to me after my father died and from the mountain of research I've done about him and that time period."

"What an interesting part he played in the war effort," Janet said. "I had no idea how animation was used until last week. And now that I know, I'm anxious to learn more."

"We both are, actually," Debbie added.

Stacy's eyes sparkled. "It's fascinating, isn't it? And I think the majority of people are like you in that they've never been told about it."

"A fact you're about to change for so many people," Janet said, smiling.

Stacy stood and motioned for Janet and Debbie to follow her. "Starting with you, Janet Shaw and Debbie Albright. There's so much I want you both to see."

Janet and Debbie eagerly trailed their hostess into the hallway and toward the rear of the house. When they reached what would have been the living room, Janet stopped in her tracks, her mouth gaping.

All around the room hung picture frames that displayed various phases of the drawing process. Some held pencil sketches of a character or a place. Some held sketches that had been partially or completely colored. And some showed a man sitting at a desk or on a bench with a sketch pad, a pencil, and a determined expression. Straight ahead and slightly off-center to the fireplace stood an antique, desk-like table with a gooseneck lamp.

"Is that the table he sat at when he worked?" Janet asked.

Stacy beamed. "It is."

Again, Janet took in the framed art all around her before smiling at Kenneth Hartman's granddaughter again. "Oh, Stacy, this is amazing."

Stacy swept her arm around the room. "Please feel free to explore. As with most art, this is best experienced up close."

Janet wandered to the first framed sketch on her left. In the center of the black-and-white picture was a young man in boxer shorts and an undershirt. An outstretched hand to his right held a uniform out to him, and an outstretched hand to his left held out a gun. The expression on the young man's face was one of uncertainty.

The next frame depicted the same young man in color, clad in his uniform with the gun held in front of him. The uncertainty he'd worn in the first drawing was gone. In its place was a mixture of determination and pride.

"Wow," Janet said as she studied both drawings. "I imagine this was used for the soldiers on the war front?"

Stacy came to stand beside Janet. "This was actually used to recruit. To help men see past their fear of the unknown and understand how they would become part of a united effort."

"I see. And after this stage, the images were redrawn onto those cel things in order to be shown as part of a film?" Janet asked.

"Exactly. These two were first used on a poster for the recruitment efforts here in the States. Later on, they were added to a sequence and turned into a film for the soldiers." Stacy pointed to a sketch pad on top of the antique desk. "The additional ones for that film are in that book. They go on to show the young man putting the uniform on, piece by piece, and being taught about the gun. In that capacity, Grandpa Ken's work was used as a training film for the soldiers."

"How fascinating," Janet said.

Stacy waved her toward the next series of drawings, which depicted radios and other pieces of wartime equipment. "Pretty much all of Grandpa Ken's work was aimed at the soldiers. Some of it was drawn to educate, and some to illustrate the things the soldiers would need to do in battle. Because of that, they were often dark and hard to watch, but they were what they needed to be for their intended audience."

"*Need It? Grow It* was outside his usual scope, wasn't it?" Janet asked.

Stacy turned wide eyes on Janet. "You know the titles of my grandfather's wartime shorts?"

"Just the one." Janet wandered over to the desk with Stacy close on her heels. "It was the first one I saw—the one that stoked my interest in wartime animation and how it was used."

Stacy touched her arm. "Where did you see it?"

"My daughter and I were helping a friend sort through some of her late mother's possessions. We came across a series of beautifully hand-drawn pictures based on *Need It? Grow It*."

"So you didn't see the finished film?"

"Actually, I did a few days later, thanks to a professor at my daughter's college. It was an honor to get to see it." Janet ran her fingers over the scarred edge of the well-used desk. "I knew, of course, that women stepped into all sorts of traditionally male jobs during that time to keep our country going. That's common knowledge, thanks to icons like Rosie the Riveter. But what drew me to that short film in particular was the reminder that even the simplest things could make a big difference during that time period."

"Growing your own food, being kind to your neighbor, and cultivating a strong work ethic in the next generation were all things people did as a matter of course back then." Stacy leaned against the wall next to the desk, her tone wistful, nostalgic for a time she'd never seen. "My maternal grandmother grew food for herself and her neighbors during the war. Grandpa Ken's mom—my great-grandmother—provided day care for the children of women in the workforce. Everyone pitched in and pulled together. Grandpa Ken even judged contests and taught workshops for those who had an interest in his field. They didn't know if animation would continue to exist if the war went badly, but he did it anyway."

Janet took in what Stacy said, her mind churning with all sorts of thoughts and questions. "It was an all-hands-on-deck time, for sure," she mused.

"It was indeed." Stacy crossed to the opposite side of the room and pointed out a small wooden plaque with her grandfather's name, KENNETH R. HARTMAN, etched across the center. "*Need It? Grow It* won Grandpa Ken his first big award in 1951. My dad found it in his attic after Grandpa Ken passed. When my dad died a few years later, Mom let me keep the award, along with all of Grandpa's sketches and cels. Most of it is his postwar animation, but I also have what he did during the war."

Janet stared at Stacy. "You have the original artwork for all of his wartime animated films?"

"I do." Stacy rubbed the plaque affectionately with her thumb then made her way back to the desk and Janet. "The original sketches in their pads, the colorized cels that were made from those drawings, and even the agreement he signed with the studio who went on to film each one. They're all going to be part of the traveling exhibit dedicated to my grandfather and his animation."

Janet shook her head in awe. "It's great that you have all of that."

"The drawings, the cels, *and* the thought process that led him to them, yes. Though the latter is in journal form inside various notebooks." Stacy rounded the corner of the antique desk and opened the top drawer. She extracted a pile of sketch pads and handed them to Janet. "These are all intact, except for the few sketches I decided to frame."

Janet held the sketch pads gingerly as Stacy closed the top drawer, opened the one below it, and removed a stack of accordion folders.

"And these are the series of colorized cels for each one," Stacy said, handing the folders to Debbie.

Janet stared from the stack of files in Debbie's arms to the sketch pads in her own, her heart galloping in her chest. "We can go through these? Really?"

"Of course. But let's do it at the kitchen table, where there's room to spread things out." Stacy led them into her bright and roomy kitchen. "Once you're done, if you'd like, I'd be happy to show you the many sketch pads and cels from his postwar stuff as well. But if I do, that might mean staying for days, on account of Grandpa Ken's long and successful career as an animator."

Janet set the sketch pads on the table, waited for Debbie to do the same with the folders, and then pulled out a chair. "While it all sounds intriguing, this is the perfect place to start for today. Thank you."

"Thank *you* for being interested enough to seek me out." Stacy opened the top sketch pad and accordion folder on each pile. "Are either of you familiar with how the animation process worked back then?"

"Not really, no," Debbie said.

"I've learned a little, but not much," Janet added.

"The artist—in this case, my grandfather—would sketch his character and its background on a piece of paper. On the next, he'd draw the same character and background with an adjustment, like an arm that's now bent or part of a uniform that he's now wearing, etc. And he'd slowly move through the story that way, a frame at a time. Then the pictures would be traced onto cels and colorized. During the filming process, the cels would be flipped at a certain speed to give the illusion of movement."

Stacy showed them each page of a story in the sketch pad and then demonstrated the movement process by flipping through the coordinating cels.

"Is this how animation is still done to this day?" Janet asked.

"The technique is similar, but much of it happens digitally now," Stacy explained as she closed the sketch pad and returned the cels to their file.

The three of them slowly made their way through Kenneth Hartman's contribution to the war effort, taking their time to admire each piece. As Tiffany, Joe Carter, and Stacy had all said, Kenneth had, in fact, skewed dark with his animation—his intended audience the soldiers fighting on the front lines. He addressed the uniforms they wore, the guns they'd use and how to properly load and fire them, what to do in the event of capture, and the importance of listening to their superior officers.

All important stuff, no doubt, but aside from the use of a cartoon to teach it, there was nothing the slightest bit lighthearted about it.

"This is all amazing, truly, but it's so very different than *Need It? Grow It*," Janet mused as Stacy closed the final sketch pad and returned its matching cels to their dedicated file. "All of these were clearly for the soldiers. Yet that one was made for those on the home front. Do you know why your grandfather chose to make that one so different from his usual work?"

"I wish I did," Stacy told her.

Janet considered the art in *Need It? Grow It*—the hardworking young woman, the inviting farmhouse in the background, the mouthwatering berries in the foreground, the sweet face of the little boy as he stared at the strawberry in the woman's hand with longing. Nothing about it matched up with Kenneth's other work, from the style to the message to the intended audience.

"I've wondered if it's because he grew tired of the heavier subject matter," she said.

"That makes sense to me," Stacy said slowly. "Guns and fighting weren't really who my grandfather was. Dark wasn't his chosen way of life."

"But he, like countless others at that time, did what needed to be done, regardless of whether it was their preference." Janet pulled the stack of sketch pads close and gently ran her hand over the top cover. "Stacy, what a thrill it's been to see these. Thank you."

"Don't you want to see your favorite?" Stacy asked.

"Yes, of course!" Janet exclaimed. "But haven't we seen all the sketch pads?"

"All of the wartime sketch pads? Yes, unfortunately." Stacy tapped the final accordion folder. "But I do have the cels for that one right here."

Stacy untied the file and carefully slid out a stack of thin plastic sheets as she had from all of the other folders. And, like before, she took the time to arrange each cel, in order, across the desk. When she was done, she spread her arms wide. "Voilà! I present to you *Need It? Grow It* in its original form."

Janet took in the work, which was becoming quite familiar to her. She studied the young woman with a blond braid in front of one shoulder and the other dangling behind her back and the white farmhouse in the distance with the set of brown rocking chairs on the front porch. She licked her lips over the juicy red strawberries, and she smiled at the little boy peering in at the strawberry with such longing. Everything was as it had been on Joe Carter's TV. The colors, the expressions, the motivation it inspired. The only difference was the lack of movement between scenes that came via the filming process.

Janet frowned at the stack of sketch pads. "So what happened to the original sketch pad for this one?"

Stacy's cheeks flushed. "That's the only one I don't have."

"That's a shame."

"Tell me about it." Stacy blew out a breath. "But at least we have the cels, right?"

Slowly, Janet examined each of the colored cels one more time, her awe at Kenneth Hartman's talent deepening. "Absolutely. I wish my daughter could be here to see them too. She'd love this behind-the-scenes look at history."

"So come back sometime. And bring her with you," Stacy said. "When you do, I'll probably have even more things to show her."

"More?" Debbie asked.

Stacy gathered the cels and returned them to their accordion folder. "The exhibit organizers thought it would be fun to include little tidbits about his thoughts, his muse, and his process. And I agree. It would be interesting for them *and* for me."

"You have that kind of information?" Debbie asked.

"I'm not sure yet. I have to do some more digging."

"Perhaps you'll come across the missing sketch pad too," Janet suggested.

Stacy pursed her lips. "That won't happen."

"Why not?"

"Someone stole it."

CHAPTER ELEVEN

S *tole* it?" Janet and Debbie echoed in shock.

"That's right. Right off his desk at the studio in the wake of his award nomination." Stacy grimaced. "That's why in the news clipping about his win, he's holding a cel in the photo instead of a paper sketch. I have it framed in the hallway. See for yourself."

She led Janet and Debbie to the framed news article. Sure enough, the drawing in Kenneth Hartman's left hand was on a cel, not paper.

"How could someone do that?" Janet cried indignantly.

"I couldn't tell you," Stacy said. "My mom, who first met my grandfather years after it happened, says it was the one part of his career that Grandpa Ken refused to discuss with anyone, even my dad. Apparently, it was a subject that upset him terribly."

"I imagine it would be very upsetting to have your work stolen," Janet said. "The time and heart he put into it, to say nothing of the award he won for it—I can't imagine losing something like that."

"From the research I've done, even the studio chose not to talk about it, opting instead to keep the focus on my grandfather's achievement with that film and the studio's own support of the war effort."

"Which was tremendous, no doubt." Janet returned to the kitchen with the others. "All of that aside, I have to agree with the people in charge of the exhibit. Being able to get inside your grandfather's thoughts from that time would be extremely fascinating."

Stacy added the closed folder to her stack and took all of them back to her grandfather's drawing desk. "If you remove the part about needing to sit in my mom's small, hot, cramped, and very disorganized attic in the hopes of doing that, I couldn't agree more."

"Yikes." Debbie chuckled as she followed Stacy with the sketch pads. "Have fun with that."

"Thanks, I think." But Stacy grinned at them.

When the files and the sketch pads were back in their respective drawers, Janet spread her arms wide to encompass the whole room. "Stacy, I can't thank you enough for allowing us to come here and see so much of your grandfather's amazing animation work. It was an honor."

"One I'm sure neither of us will ever forget," Debbie added.

"It was my pleasure. Truly."

"We should probably head out," Janet said regretfully.

"You're welcome back anytime," Stacy assured her. "Don't forget your purse."

"Right. Thank you." Janet scooped up her bag, rummaged inside it for her business cards, and handed one to Stacy. "If you need help getting things together for the exhibit, give me a call. I'd love to work on this with you."

"Thank you." Stacy pocketed the card and led them through the house to the front door. "You may find yourself wishing you hadn't offered."

"No, I won't. We've had a lovely time this evening." Janet trailed Debbie through the door Stacy held open and then faced her hostess. "Good night, Stacy. And thank you again. Your pride in your grandfather is a beautiful thing."

"I couldn't feel any different about him if I tried," Stacy said.

As she climbed into her car for the drive home, Janet knew the young woman had been telling the truth.

It was a shame about that missing sketch pad, though—

And then Janet had a thought that made her blood run cold.

Janet had just finished loading the dishwasher when Debbie stepped into the kitchen and released a long sigh. From anyone else, that act in that moment would be one of exhaustion or relief or some combination of both. From Debbie, the sigh was one of joy after another successful day doing what they'd set out to do together.

Willing her expression to mirror the one she knew Debbie wore, Janet started the day's final load of dishes and immediately busied herself cleaning the nearby countertops. "Closed sign up?"

"It is."

"Another good day?" Janet asked.

"It sure was."

"Fantastic." She worked the cloth around the handles of the kitchen faucet and then moved on to the latest layer of flour coating her workspace. "Two more days, and then we get one off."

"Thank goodness. I have a feeling I'll need it."

"Any plans for after church on Sunday?" Janet swapped out her used cloth for a clean one and did a second pass over the space.

"Not yet."

She surveyed her work, decided the counter was done, and crossed to the stove. A pass around the burners and another around the trim of all three ovens gave her time to intentionally slow her breathing the way she had countless times that day. "You can head out. I don't have much left to do before—"

"Stop."

Janet paused the cloth on the handle of the top oven, her back to Debbie.

"Put the cloth down and talk to me, Janet."

Slowly, she lowered the cloth to her side. "I've been talking," she said, keeping her tone light.

"Yes, but you haven't said anything."

Janet blew out a breath and faced her friend, though she had to avoid Debbie's piercing gaze. "Okay. I'm listening."

"No, *I'm* listening. *You're* talking." Debbie leaned her shoulder against the wall. "Which you did very little of on the way home from Stacy's last night."

Janet slumped back against the oven and blew out another, longer breath. "I was tired, you were tired. It was late."

"No doubt. But it's the next day, and you're still quiet."

"It's been a busy day," Janet said.

"It's more than that." Debbie peered at Janet. "And for what it's worth, I'm wondering the same thing."

"About what?"

"Those pictures you and Tiffany found in Audrey's mother's box."

Janet fidgeted. "What about them?"

Debbie raised an eyebrow at her but said nothing.

Janet scowled and tossed the dirty cloths into the hamper then lifted out the hamper bag and closed it for the drive home. "They can't be the ones that were stolen," she murmured. "They just can't. Audrey adored her mother. It would destroy her."

Debbie hurried to her side, took the hamper bag from her and set it on the ground then tugged Janet out into the dining area. When they were both settled at the counter, Debbie took a deep breath. "Let's talk out what we know," she said.

And so they did. They discussed their visit with Stacy, her pride in her grandfather's work, and animated shorts. And then they talked about the first-step drawings in the sketch pads and the colorized versions on the cels.

"It was so fun for me to see how the films Joe Carter showed me in his office last week actually started," Janet added. "Tiffany would have loved it."

"Let's talk about the elephant in the room, Janet." Debbie pinned her with a firm gaze. "Stacy has the original sketches as well as the colorized cels for every one of her grandfather's animated wartime shorts—except one. For that one, she has only the cels. Because the sketches were stolen."

Janet stared at the large window on the far wall. "And quite possibly found in a storage area last week."

"I didn't see them, so I can't know if that's actually a possibility."

Janet leaned her elbows on the counter, buried her face in her hands, and groaned. "It could very well be possible."

"They're that good?" Debbie asked.

"They're that good. They're spot-on for the cels we saw. I thought they were made by a dedicated student." Janet stared down at the counter. "And now I can't get the possibility that they might be the originals out of my head."

Janet got up and wandered over to one of the windows responsible for filling the room with sunlight. She closed her eyes, lifted her face to the midafternoon warmth, and willed it to chase away the persistent chill she'd felt all day.

"How old was Audrey's mother during the war?" Debbie asked.

Janet opened her eyes to find Debbie watching her with a troubled expression. "I'm not sure. A young teenager, I think?" She managed to croak her words past the lump that had taken up residence in her throat for much of the day.

"And she lived where?"

"She grew up on a farm, but I'm not sure where. The Midwest, I'm guessing."

For a few long minutes, neither of them said anything.

Finally, Debbie stood and joined Janet at the window. "I'm not sure how feasible it would have been for a girl in her early teens to steal sketches from an art studio."

There was no denying the hope borne on her friend's words—or how quickly it faded with Janet's counterpoint. "They were stolen *after* the war, remember? In 1951. Right after Stacy's grandfather was nominated for his award. Audrey's mother would have been older then."

Janet watched a pair of teenagers walking a dog past the window. Normally, the sight would have made her smile, but she couldn't today. "And if they *are* the stolen sketches, they should be with Stacy, not Audrey."

"They should be."

"But what would that do to Audrey?" Janet asked. "Audrey's best friend was her mother. They did everything together and told each other everything."

Debbie perched on the edge of a nearby table. "She didn't know about the pictures in her mother's box, right?"

"Right. And it was obvious that they threw her for a loop," Janet said.

"Okay, I get that. But the groundwork is laid now, don't you think? That her mother didn't tell her everything after all?"

Janet considered Debbie's words but dismissed them with the same reality that had tortured her throughout the day. "Not knowing about something's existence is one thing. Learning something that could change the way you see someone who's important to you is entirely different."

"I didn't think of it that way," Debbie admitted.

Janet massaged her temples. "Audrey adored her mother, Debbie. It's been two years since Mae passed, and Audrey still can't bring herself to go through her personal things yet. Every time her mother comes up in conversation, the pain on Audrey's face is undeniable. How can we risk adding something worse to her grief?"

"Oh, Janet…" The same anguish Janet had felt since the night before was evident in Debbie's voice.

"Exactly. That's why I've been so quiet all day today," Janet said. "And it's why I spent more time staring up at the ceiling last night than I did actually sleeping."

"What do we do about this?" Debbie asked.

It was a good question. It was also one Janet couldn't answer, despite the many times she'd repeated it.

"I don't know," she said miserably.

Debbie stood and pulled Janet in for a hug. "Pray on it, my friend. And I will too. For His wisdom to quiet your heart and show you the best course of action."

"Me?"

"I'm here for you every step of the way. You know that. But I didn't find the pictures, and I haven't spent time with Audrey like you have. You need to take point on this one."

"You're right." Janet gave her friend an extra squeeze and stepped back. "Now, I think I've held up your departure long enough, don't you? So scoot. I'll grab the laundry bag and be on my way soon too."

"You must be exhausted, Janet. Why don't you let me take the laundry today and tomorrow, and you can take it over the weekend?" Debbie suggested.

Janet lifted her hand. "No, I've got it. I can use the time it's in the washing machine to sneak in a little nap."

"You sure?"

Janet grinned, grateful for such a thoughtful friend and business partner. "I'm sure. Now go. Please. I don't need guilt on top of worry right now."

"No guilt," Debbie said, backing her way toward the office. "I'm going. See you—wait a second."

Janet planted her hands on her hips. "Now what?"

"I have an idea for Ian's birthday gift."

"You do?" Janet didn't know what she'd expected her friend to say, but it wasn't that.

"It was Greg's idea, but I think it's a good one."

Janet felt her left eyebrow shoot up. "Greg?"

A slight pinking of Debbie's cheeks preceded her answering nod. "It came up last night."

"Over another ice cream date?"

"No. Outside my house after dinner. He was walking Hammer with Julian." Hammer was Greg's border collie and almost constant companion.

"Past your house?"

"Yes."

"I see," Janet said between failed attempts to stop grinning.

"Julian has a friend who lives on the end of my street," Debbie said defensively. "So Greg parked outside my house. He thought it would make for some good exercise for all three of them. Hammer needed it anyway."

Janet's grin turned into a full-fledged smile, her first of the day. "This is really happening between you two."

"Now I know for sure how tired you are." But Debbie's eye roll held no true irritation. "Do you want to hear the idea or not?"

"I'd love to."

"He suggested an impact screen for the basement that Ian can hit golf balls into. It might be a good way to blow off steam, which Ian might appreciate, considering his job as police chief."

Janet took the idea in and let it simmer. "I suppose that could work. He doesn't play golf, and he doesn't have any clubs, but it's possible he would if he had the opportunity."

"That was my thought as well."

Janet pulled Debbie in for a quick yet happy hug. "Thank you so much. I needed an idea like this. And please thank Greg the next time you see him."

The pink hue was back in Debbie's cheeks as she stepped away. "I will, of course. But I don't know when that'll be. Church on Sunday, I guess."

"Or tonight, if Julian simply must visit his friend again," Janet suggested, grinning.

Debbie grinned. "I hope he must."

"You and me, both, my friend. You and me both. Anyway, go on now. I'll take care of the last few things that need to be done here, and then I'll be on my way too." Janet walked Debbie to the door. "And thank you again. For sharing the idea for Ian, for going with me last night, and for talking it all through with me just now. I'm a long way from knowing the best way to approach this whole thing with the sketches, but you're right—we'll figure it out. With God's help."

"Not a doubt in my mind," Debbie sang out as she left the café.

Janet watched her go. It was a sticky situation for sure, but there was no one else she'd rather have in it with her.

CHAPTER TWELVE

She was waiting outside when Ian pulled into the driveway the next day. Beside her sat two water bottles, and on her feet were a pair of sneakers.

"Why are you sitting out here?" Ian called through the window as he shifted into park and cut the engine.

Grabbing the water bottles, Janet stood. "Waiting for you."

The cleft in Ian's chin deepened with his smile. "Don't I feel special?"

"You should, because you are." She made her way to his car and leaned through the window to kiss him.

Ian pointed at her shirt as she stepped back. "Plaid? That's not like you."

She tugged at the shirt she'd picked up on the way home from the café. "When in Rome, you know."

"They wear plaid in Rome?" Ian teased.

She kissed him again and then tossed the water bottles past him and onto the passenger seat. "Golfers wear plaid."

The sparkle in her husband's eyes was temporarily muted with confusion. "Golfers?"

"Yup. I checked pictures on the internet to be sure."

"Okay. But you don't golf."

"I'm thinking it might be good for you," she said.

His smile faded. "Me?"

"Yes. To blow off steam. It's something you could do with your friends after work or on a Saturday. Maybe even with me from time to time, if I'm not too horrible at it." Janet rounded the front of the car and opened the passenger door. "But I guess I'll know that after we go to the driving range over in Uhrichsville."

He stared at her as she transferred the water bottles from the seat to the cup holders and sat down. "You want to go to a driving range right now?"

She nodded. "It's Friday. You're off tomorrow. Why not?"

"I don't golf, Janet."

"I know. But you should change that."

Ian twisted in his seat to face her. "I don't *want* to change that."

"But it would be good for you."

"To blow off steam?" he asked.

"Yes, with your friends and sometimes me."

He held up his hands. "I don't need to blow off steam, Janet. I told you before, this is Dennison, not New York City. Our calls at the department aren't all that taxing. But when the occasional one is, I'm able to work through it. And when I'm not working and you're not working, I want to spend my time with *you*, not the guys."

She felt her whole body deflate. "We could golf together."

"Is that really what you want?" he asked.

She sat with his question for a moment then sighed. "No."

"Thank goodness."

With one last glance down at her plaid shirt, Janet gathered up the water bottles and reached for the door handle. "I should probably let you go inside. I'm sure you're tired from your day."

"Any tiredness I felt disappeared as soon as I pulled in and saw you waiting for me."

She smiled. "I'm glad."

"Good. Now I want to do something together," he said, stilling her departure with his hand on her arm. "So put the water bottles back down and buckle up."

"Where are we going?"

"It's a nice day." He faced forward in his seat and started the car again. "The sun is shining. It's a little warm. And my wife is cute in her plaid shirt."

Her laugh mingled with his. "Cute?"

"Cute," he repeated with conviction. "So I'm taking her out for ice cream."

"Ice cream?" Janet echoed. "But we haven't eaten dinner yet."

Ian shifted into reverse and looked behind them as he backed onto the street. "You're right, we haven't. I won't tell your parents."

"Tiffany spent the day with Ashling, and she's not home yet."

"She knows how to cook if she's hungry. This is a date." He turned the wheel and shifted into drive. "We can bring her a cup of her favorite if you want."

"I think she'd have our heads if we didn't."

"You're probably right." He drove down the street, the familiar houses and businesses passing by her window. "Was it my imagination, or did you get out of bed before your alarm this morning?"

Her gaze still on the passing scenery, she shifted in her seat. "A little before, I guess."

"And you didn't come back to bed."

She avoided his gaze. "I was having trouble sleeping, and I figured I might as well be productive. So I cleaned the refrigerator."

"The refrigerator?"

"I've been meaning to get to it for a while now. This morning seemed like as good a time as any."

"You need sleep, Janet."

"And so do you," she said. "My tossing and turning next to you would have affected that."

He released a hand from the steering wheel to wave aside her concern. "If you aren't feeling well or you're troubled by something, I want to know about it."

"It wasn't a question of not feeling well." She gazed at their church as they drove by, the parking lot empty on a Friday evening.

"My keen power of deduction tells me something was on your mind."

"It still is. But as Debbie said, I just need to pray on it, and it will all work out, even if I can't see how yet."

Ian pulled into the gravel lot by the pastel awning of their favorite ice-cream shop. "Is this about your birthday gift debacle? Because if it is, you need to stop."

"I can't. It matters to me. But clearly something golf-related isn't the answer I'd hoped it would be."

"Janet, I don't need or want anything other than who and what God has already blessed me with. Losing sleep trying to convince yourself otherwise is foolish."

She took in the handful of people scattered around the shop benches and tables. "As far as last night was concerned, my thoughts were all over the place. Otherwise, I probably could have slept better."

"Why didn't you wake me?" Ian asked. "I might have been able to help."

"I needed to think, process, play things out."

"And now?" he asked as he cut the engine.

"We can talk about that. But *after* I get my ice cream."

"Priorities." His hearty laugh accompanied them out of the car and up to the window where they placed their orders—a small cup of vanilla ice cream with butterscotch sauce for her, and a large vanilla with brownie bites and hot fudge for him.

When their order was ready, they meandered over to an empty bench in a less-populated corner and sat. For a few moments, they simply enjoyed their treats.

Eventually, though, Ian pointed his spoon at Janet. "Is this about your trip to Pittsburgh the other night?"

She looked down at her remaining ice cream and felt her appetite disappear. "Remember those drawings Tiffany and I found when we went through Audrey's storage area? The ones Tiffany and her professor both thought were copied from a World War II animated short?"

Nodding, he took another bite.

"After my visit with the animator's granddaughter, I'm beginning to think they aren't copies."

He spooned up a brownie piece. "So they weren't as close to the original as Tiffany thought?"

"No, they're close." Janet lifted her cup and dug in her spoon but then set the whole thing back down. "Dead-on, actually."

He started to take another bite but paused, waiting for her to say more. When she didn't, he turned so his knees touched hers. "I think I'm lost. You said you didn't think those pictures you found in

Audrey's mother's things were copied from the animator's short. And now, you're saying the complete opposite."

"You're not lost," she said. "That's exactly what I'm saying."

"What do you mean by that?"

"The original sketches Kenneth Hartman did for *Need It? Grow It* were stolen over fifty years ago," she said.

His confusion morphed into understanding. "You think the sketches you and Tiffany found could be the originals?"

"I don't know for sure. I mean, I don't have any evidence. But they are alarmingly good."

"Oh. Wow."

"There's no doubt in my mind that Audrey had never seen them before," Janet said quickly. "I believe that a hundred percent. But she said that she and her mother, Mae, were best friends. That they told each other everything."

"Yet she didn't know about the pictures or why they were in her mother's things." Ian gave a long, low whistle.

Janet slumped against the bench. "If Mae stole them, it would certainly explain why she didn't tell Audrey about them."

"It would, but is it possible that someone else put them in Mae's things and even Mae didn't know?"

Janet drew back. "Someone else? Like who?"

"There's no telling at this stage. I'm just floating the possibility." Ian took another bite of ice cream. "Or, if Mae knew, is it possible she had them to protect the person who actually stole them?"

She considered his words, the tension in her shoulders easing a fraction. "I assumed, since they were in Mae's things, that she was behind the theft. Perhaps it's not so cut-and-dried."

Ian nudged her. "This is why you wake me instead of getting out of bed to clean the refrigerator. Agreed?"

"Agreed." She picked up her ice cream cup and drank its melted contents. "If they are the stolen sketches, I don't want it to be Audrey's mom who stole them. Because if that's what happened, it'll destroy the way Audrey sees her mom. She's gone through enough. She doesn't deserve that."

"I would imagine you're right." He finished his ice cream, took her cup, and then carried both containers to the closest trash can. "So, what are you going to do?"

"Want to walk a little?" she suggested, standing.

"Sure. We'll work off some of that."

They stepped onto a dirt path that led from the rear of the ice cream shop to a small pond. As they walked, Ian draped his arm across her shoulders, the way he tended to do when she was troubled. And as usual, the weight of his arm seemed to convey some of his calm to her.

"I wish I could go back to the ignorance I had about all of this before I took that drive. But I can't," Janet said. "I want the pictures Tiffany and I found to be a coincidence—just copies, as we previously thought. But if they're the stolen originals, Stacy has a right to those images. They're her grandfather's work, his legacy, and a link to his past."

Ian guided her to the edge of the pond, to a large rock perfectly sized for two people. He patted the almost-flat surface, but Janet remained standing, her mind too active for her to stay still.

"So I'm guessing you're going to talk to Audrey? Pose the possibility that they may be the stolen sketches?" he asked.

She gazed toward the center of the pond and the pair of ducks lazily floating in the sun's waning rays. "I think I have to, don't you?"

"I do."

Janet watched the ducks paddle to the far end of the pond. "If you found out your mother committed a crime like this, would you be able to keep that one wrong from ruining everything else you knew about her?"

Ian scrubbed at his stubbled jawline as he pondered her question. "It would be hard at first. But I think, in time, I'd find my way back to the person I knew and loved, the goodness I'd witnessed, and the many truths she'd shown me."

"Would that be enough?"

"I'd learn to make it so," he said.

How she loved this man. His levelheadedness, his ability to listen, his willingness to see different angles, and the way he said exactly what she needed to hear were such a blessing.

"I love you, Ian."

Pushing off the rock, he pulled her close. "And that, my love, is the best present—birthday or otherwise—I could ever ask for."

"You're going to get a real present," she said. "Somehow, some-way, I will figure one out that will blow your socks off."

"But I don't want anything. I really—"

Janet reached up and pressed her finger to his lips. "A birthday gift is not open for debate, Chief."

"Whatever you say."

CHAPTER THIRTEEN

Janet closed the oven and set an additional minute on her timer as the kitchen door swung open to admit Debbie. "The apple cinnamon muffins need a bit longer, and then they'll be good to go."

"Perfect." Debbie hooked her thumb at the door and stepped toward her, lowering her voice. "Audrey is here."

Janet froze. "A to-go order?"

Debbie closed the remaining gap between them. "No. She's sitting at the table in the far corner with a cup of coffee and a piece of chocolate cream pie, and she looks pretty lonely."

"I see."

"She'd probably love it if you came out to say hi," Debbie said.

Janet felt her shoulders droop. "Normally I would, but how can I keep what we know from her? I'm not ready to talk to her about it yet."

Debbie laid a hand on Janet's shoulder and squeezed. "You'll figure out the right thing to do."

The timer went off. "Okay. As soon as I take care of these muffins, I'll go out there and say hello."

"And?" Debbie prompted.

Janet opened the oven door and transferred the pan of golden-brown muffins to the top of the stove. "And I'll see how the conversation goes. If she's having a sad day for some reason, I'll wait to approach the subject of the drawings. If she's not, then I'll say something, if I can muster up the courage and figure out the right words to use." She nodded at the muffins. "I have to get the topping on these while they're still warm."

"I can get those from here." Debbie shooed Janet away from the muffins. "I have no doubt you'll make the right call. Now go."

"Thanks, I think." Janet tugged off her oven mitts, placed them on the counter beside the muffin trays, and hung her apron on its hook. With a deep breath, she squared her shoulders. "Here I go."

When she stepped out into the dining area, Janet's gaze immediately traveled to the far corner and the now-familiar face staring down into a coffee cup. Beside the cup sat an empty plate and a fork.

The part of Janet that hated seeing people sad urged her to hurry to Audrey's table and make everything better. But the part of her that loathed even the possibility of hurting someone wanted to retreat to the kitchen.

The decision was made for her when Audrey glanced up and waved.

There was no going back now. Janet made her way across the café. "Audrey, hello. Happy Saturday."

"Happy Saturday, Janet." Audrey pointed at her empty plate. "Your chocolate cream pie was calling to me as soon as I woke up this morning. I answered the call."

Janet sat in the chair across from her. "Sometimes I think our bodies tell us what they need."

"I'm not sure a body ever truly *needs* chocolate cream pie," Audrey said, laughing. "My soul? Clearly. My body? Probably not."

Janet took in the tiny crumbs that remained on the plate and then forced herself to appraise her new friend's expression. Her smile didn't quite reach her eyes, which appeared a little dull.

"Are you okay?" Janet asked.

Audrey's smile faltered. "I'm trying to be. I'm doing what all the magazine articles say to do to make yourself happy. I'm playing music and singing along. I'm getting my fingers into the dirt in my yard and planting things. I'm going for walks and taking deep breaths. I'm treating myself to things that make me happy, as you can see."

"But?"

"But I'm starting to wonder if I made a mistake with this move," Audrey said, toying with her fork.

Janet scooted forward in her seat. "Oh, don't think that, Audrey. Dennison is a wonderful place to live. You just need to meet more people. Once you do, I have no doubt you'll love it here."

"It's not the town, Janet. And although I haven't met many people, the few I have met have all been very nice and made me feel so welcome."

"You'll meet more, Audrey, I promise," Janet said. "At church, here at the café, and when you're out and about—especially now that summer is right around the corner."

Audrey finished her coffee and then pushed the mug into the center of the table along with her empty plate. "It's not the people either."

"Then what is it?" Janet asked.

Audrey bit her lip before speaking again. "I moved because I thought a new place would help me focus on the future rather than the past. But now that I have the new place, I miss the memories, the familiarity, and—well, *her*."

"Your mom."

Audrey's answering nod was heavy. "We lived together every day of my life. First as a child, in our house in Indiana, until my father died when I was twenty-three, and then in adulthood, in the house I bought outside of Cincinnati. Her memory was everywhere in that house, and it was tied to everything inside it too."

Janet tried to swallow back the lump in her throat as Audrey spoke, but to no avail. She couldn't imagine that kind of grief.

"Yet, here in Dennison, those memories are nowhere," Audrey said. "Nothing feels like her. And somehow that's worse."

Silently resolving to call her own mother at the next opportunity, Janet did her best to speak without a quiver in her voice. "She's still here in you, Audrey. You're her daughter. You carry a piece of her with you wherever you go. And she lives on in your memories, right?"

Audrey's throat moved with a swallow. "Yes."

"I do have an idea for you to consider. What if you take some of her things and set them up around the house so it feels like she's in the new place too?" Janet asked. "Like the things you associate most with her."

A hint of pink colored Audrey's cheeks. "That would mean I'd have to actually go through her boxes. I still haven't."

"What's holding you back?" Janet asked gently.

"It's silly, really. Tiffany put them exactly where I asked her to. Yet here we are, a week and a half later, and they're still in that same exact place—still taped, still untouched. At night, when I wonder why I haven't gotten to them, I tell myself it's because whatever else I did that day was more pressing. But I know that's not true. The truth is that I keep putting it off because I know it's going to be painful."

"Is there any chance some of the things in those boxes belonged to other family members?" Janet asked.

Audrey tilted her head in thought. "You mean that she inherited?"

"Right. Like heirlooms from other relatives."

"I know she treasured a necklace from her grandmother and a shiny pebble her favorite brother, Everett, brought back to her from the war," Audrey said. "Mama showed them both to me over the years. I'm sure they'll be in with her things somewhere—probably inside the little wooden trinket box her uncle made for her tenth birthday."

A favorite brother? An uncle?

Maybe Ian was right and Mae hadn't done anything wrong after all.

"Who boxed up her stuff after she passed?" Janet asked.

"No one. Mama had already packed it all up a good twenty years earlier in preparation for some work I had done in my attic. I wanted to help because I always loved seeing pieces of her childhood and hearing the stories that went along with them, but I was working crazy hours at the hospital back then and didn't have time. I wish I'd made the time now. My brother came over and helped for a few hours once or twice, but Mama pretty much did it all alone."

Janet pursed her lips. "Your brother?"

"Yes. Larry. I told you about him, remember? He was an accountant in New York and died about ten years ago. Once the attic work was done, Mama opted to leave everything packed. Said she'd done a good enough job packing that if she needed something, she'd know which box to find it in."

Leaning forward, Janet patted Audrey's hand. "Would it help to have someone there with you when you go through them?"

"I don't have anyone to ask," Audrey said glumly. "I'm the last of the Barkers."

"You can ask me."

Audrey stared at Janet. "I can't ask you to do that."

"I'm happy to volunteer if you think it would help. And it would give us a chance to talk more."

Audrey's eyes grew misty. "I don't know what to say."

"Would it help?" Janet prodded.

Audrey's agreement was so quiet that Janet had to lean forward to hear it. But it was there, along with the hope that had quietly traded places with sadness on her face.

"How about Monday? Say, around four o'clock?"

"Monday at four would be wonderful," Audrey said. "If you're sure you don't mind."

"I don't mind at all. I'll consider it a privilege."

Audrey placed her hand on top of Janet's. "Thank you. For letting me hire Tiffany. For inviting me to church this past Sunday and introducing me to people at the doughnut breakfast afterward. For your kindness every time I see you. And for offering to be with me while I go through my mother's things. For everything, honestly."

"It's my pleasure. Truly," Janet replied, even as guilt sank like a stone in her stomach. How could she truly be Audrey's friend and suspect something so awful about her family?

Audrey scooted off her chair and onto her feet. "I've taken far too much of your time already, so I'll leave you to the rest of your day. Besides, your visit on Monday has given me a reason to get back to unpacking and organizing my own things. After we go through Mama's boxes, I would appreciate it if you could help me decide what to do with her stuff."

"You mean like what you should keep and what you should give away?"

"Yes. Also, decisions about things like that set of drawings you and Tiffany found. Should I get them bound into some sort of book, or should I frame a few of them and hang them in the extra bedroom?"

Janet willed her expression and tone to remain neutral. Like it or not, she would have to share her suspicions about the pictures with Audrey on Monday when they were together. "I'm not sure off the top of my head, but let me think about it between now and then."

"Okay. I'm still flabbergasted about the pictures. How my mother came to have them and why she never told me about them. But I can't know those answers without her being here to tell me." Audrey scooped up her purse from the back of her chair. "Still, if they meant enough for her to hang on to them, they clearly mattered to her. Which means they now matter to me."

How Janet wished that were the case—that the set of drawings she and Tiffany had found among Mae Barker's personal things were truly nothing more than a welcome link between a grieving daughter and her beloved late mother. There was certainly a chance they could be, but until Janet knew for sure, she had to be careful with what she said.

Audrey slung her purse over her shoulder. "I'll see you Monday at four o'clock. I live at 12 Morningside Court."

"Monday at four," Janet repeated. "Got it."

"Thank you again." And then, with a bounce in her step, Audrey made her way through the café door while Janet stared after her.

What had she gotten herself into?

CHAPTER FOURTEEN

After a busy Sunday, Janet tried to sleep, she really did, but she spent more than an hour staring up at the ceiling and then gave up. After slipping into her robe and slippers, she looked back at the bed, envying her husband's ability to put everything out of his mind when it came time to sleep.

She wished she could do the same, but for her, bedtime had always been a time to think about all the things she'd been too busy to think about during the day. Like the laundry she still needed to do, the calls she'd intended to make but hadn't, the recipe that hadn't worked as well as she'd hoped and how she could fix it, the committee meeting she'd agreed to when she really shouldn't have, and anything and everything to do with Ian and Tiffany.

She softly padded out of the room and into the hall. She would go to the pantry and organize the third shelf and perhaps her thoughts at the same time. But as she moved in that direction, a sliver of light under Tiffany's partially open door stole all thoughts of alphabetizing soup cans.

"Tiffany?" Janet whispered, peeking in at her daughter. "You're still up?"

"I am."

Janet stepped into the carpeted room. Her daughter—Ian's double in everything from the cleft in her chin to the widow's peak in her auburn hair—sat on her bed with her laptop.

Tiffany patted the spot beside her on the bed. "Come see what I've found for Dad."

"For Dad?" Janet repeated.

"Kind of. But it's more for you and your sanity."

Janet quietly pushed the door closed and joined Tiffany on the bed. "What do you mean?"

"Come on, Mom. I'd have to be blind not to see how preoccupied you've been all weekend. I thought instead of giving you a hard time about Dad's present, I should try to help." Tiffany's fingers flew over the keyboard. "So, I've come up with an idea. We know Dad isn't into *stuff*. He just isn't. And that's why any *stuff* you get him will likely stay in the box, untouched. So I think giving him a gift to do something would be better."

"That was Debbie's idea too. Or, rather, Greg's thought that Debbie shared with me. But it fell flat."

Tiffany grinned at her. "Yeah, I heard about that. Dad and golf? Those two things don't go together. Except in the punch line of a joke."

"In my defense, I thought that if we went to a driving range together, he'd enjoy it," Janet said, settling back against the headboard. "Then I could've swooped in with lessons or something for his birthday."

"At least you got some ice cream for your effort, right?" Tiffany tapped a few more keys. "By the way, I'm still bummed I didn't get any."

Janet leaned in for a peek at the screen but saw only pop-up windows with cars and boats and...*corn mazes?* "We intended to bring you some. We really did. But we got distracted talking by the pond, and then we forgot. It won't happen again."

"I'll hold you to that." Tiffany pointed at the image of the blue-and-white race car she'd enlarged in the center of her screen. "Okay, so there's a place in the Akron area where you can drive a race car on a real racetrack. Do you think Dad might enjoy doing something like that?"

A quiet thrill ran up Janet's spine at the possibility. "Hey, that's not a bad idea at all."

"For an additional fee, you could do it with him," Tiffany said. "Which would probably make him enjoy it even more."

Janet held up her hands. "Me in a race car? Not a chance. But he could take one of his friends."

"It's expensive though, so we might want to find out whether it's something he'd even want to do before you actually buy it."

"I want him to be surprised by whatever I get him," Janet protested. "Asking him about it would ruin that."

Tiffany eyed Janet with an amused expression. "Okay, but if you hadn't tried to get him to go golfing, you might have paid for lessons he wouldn't want. Do you want to risk that here?"

"True." Janet studied the race car on the screen. "So I'll find a way to ask him without actually asking him."

Tiffany clapped a hand over her mouth to stifle her laughter. "Which we both know you can't do."

"I can be subtle," Janet said.

"With some things, sure. But there's no way you can ask Dad about something as random as driving a race car. I think I might do a better job."

She started to argue then thought better of it. "You're probably right. But I need you to find out tomorrow so I have time to keep searching if he feels about this the way he does about golf."

Tiffany minimized the picture of the race car. "There are lots of experiences we can look into if the race-car thing falls flat. Like bungee jumping, or zip-lining. All sorts of things."

Janet took in the assortment of pictures on the screen and then smiled at her daughter. "Thanks for checking into these things for me. It's a big help, especially with how scattered I've been lately. I haven't even been able to think about what to get him since the golf debacle."

Tiffany raised an eyebrow. "Wait. Are you saying you weren't stressing over what to get Dad last night during dinner and then again after church today, at our picnic in the park?"

"That's right."

Tiffany closed her computer. "Is there something you're not telling me? You were so clearly somewhere else both times."

"It's nothing, really."

"Mom, I'm not a little girl anymore."

She played with the end of Tiffany's braid. "If you were, you'd have been asleep four hours ago."

"Talk to me, Mom."

So she did. She gave her more details about the visit with Stacy Hartman and the aspects of Kenneth Hartman's career she'd gotten to see while she was there—the pictures, the original sketches, the cels, and the drawing desk.

Then she told Tiffany about the one sketch pad that wasn't there and why.

"It was *stolen?*" Tiffany echoed. "Wow. That's awful."

"I know." Janet twisted her hands in her lap. "And if one of my scenarios is right, I'm worried about the effect it'll have on Audrey."

Tiffany scrunched her nose in confusion. "Why would she care one way or the other about…"

When Tiffany's sentence trailed off, Janet knew her daughter had caught up to the part of the story she'd yet to explain. The horror that crossed Tiffany's face was simply added confirmation.

"Oh no," Tiffany said. "Mom, tell me that's not what happened."

"I don't know why Audrey's mom would've stolen them or how she'd even have access to steal them, but it's a very real possibility without more information, which she can't give us," Janet said. "And if not Audrey's mom, then someone else inside her family may have done it, and her mother didn't want anyone to know. I have no idea how to break such news to Audrey. But keeping it to myself isn't fair to Stacy if those drawings are in fact her grandfather's."

Tiffany said nothing at first, the expression on her face letting Janet know her daughter was processing. "Why didn't you tell me about this sooner?" she finally asked.

"And ruin the fun of discovering those drawings together?" Janet replied. "I didn't want to take anything away from you either, Tiffany."

"I deserve the truth, Mom, no matter how tough it is. Tell me about the sketch pads that went with his other wartime shorts."

Janet straightened, recalling the living room Stacy had devoted to her grandfather's legacy. "She had them all, except for *Need It? Grow It*, and it was fun going through each one. Occasionally I'd see an erasure mark indicating a change in direction for a character or setting, and I could imagine him sitting at his desk, giving life to whatever image he had in his head."

"What about the cels that went with them?" Tiffany asked.

"Those were so interesting. The pencil sketches were already vivid and exciting, but the addition of color made the stories come to life in a whole different way."

Tiffany grew quiet for a moment while Janet gave in to a welcome yawn. "So, they all held to the normal animation process?"

"Meaning?" Janet asked after another yawn.

"Like the first phase was the pencil sketch and the second phase was the colorized version on the cel."

"From what I could see, yes."

"And all the sketches Stacy showed you were like that? Free of color?"

Janet grabbed her daughter's arm. "You're right! The pictures we found in Audrey's mother's box were all fully colored." Pulling Tiffany in for a tight hug, Janet felt every knot in her own body loosen. "Thank you so much. I've been so worried about what to say to Audrey and how that would affect her feelings about her mother."

"You're welcome." Tiffany leaned back to grin at her. "This is why you should've waited for me before going out for ice cream. If you had, this stuff would have all come out then, and I could have saved you the past two days of being all stressed about something other than Dad's birthday."

Janet stifled her answering laugh. "Point received, lesson learned."

"Good. And now, one last thing before you go?"

"What's that?"

"Where's your necklace? I thought you had it on last week, but I haven't seen it since."

She'd completely forgotten to tell Tiffany what had happened. "The clasp broke at work the other day, and I haven't made it to the jewelers in New Philly yet to get it fixed. But I will. I promise."

"It's not a huge deal, Mom."

Janet smiled at her. "It is to me. Just like you are. Now I need to get some sleep."

Tiffany chuckled. "I hope you can now."

Janet headed back to bed, her heart lighter than it had been in days.

CHAPTER FIFTEEN

*J*anet shut off her car outside the small but inviting bungalow at 12 Morningside Court and eyed her dashboard clock with immense satisfaction. Despite a few straggling customers and her usual checklist of closing tasks, she'd still managed to get to Audrey's on time. With her friend's favorite pie in a white box on the passenger seat to boot.

Smiling at the knowledge that her plans for the visit no longer included breaking Audrey's heart, Janet scooped up the box, pushed open her car door, and made her way up the walk.

The navy blue door swung open as she reached it.

"You found me," Audrey said brightly.

"I did. Your directions were perfect." Janet accepted the hug Audrey offered and then held out the bakery box. "I took a chance on which pie you might enjoy."

Her brown eyes widening, Audrey peeked into the box and laughed. "You didn't have to bring me a whole pie."

"Sure I did. It's an overdue housewarming gift." Janet stepped back to admire the front of Audrey's bungalow then the ones on either side of it. "I saw a few billboards about this independent-living neighborhood when they were building it, but this is the first time I've actually been here. It's really nice."

Audrey glanced up from the pie and looked out at the houses across from her own as if seeing them for the first time. "You think so?"

"Absolutely. The whole neighborhood gives off a very welcoming vibe, and I think I was waved to more in the last block than I've been waved at on my own street in the past week."

"People *do* seem friendly," Audrey acknowledged with a shrug.

Janet pointed in the direction she'd come. "What's that white building inside the front gate, the one with the parking lot?"

"That's the activities building. It's where residents get together to play cards, craft, visit with one another, and, on Friday evenings, sit around an outdoor firepit to eat s'mores and sing campfire songs. It also has a lending library from what I was told when I was checking the place out to decide whether to buy."

"You had me at s'mores and library," Janet joked. "With all those opportunities, it sounds like you should have no problem meeting people."

Audrey's smile slipped from her face. "If I actually left my house."

"You leave," Janet protested. "You've been to the café a few times. And church."

"And that's all I've done," Audrey said. "Besides trips to the grocery store."

"But we're going to change that, right?"

"I don't know. I know I should want to. But knowing and doing are proving to be two very different things for me these days." Pasting her smile back in place, Audrey waved Janet inside. "Like inviting you here and then making you stand outside. I'm sorry.

I don't know where my head is half the time. Please come in. I'll serve the pie and make coffee if you'd like some."

"Yes, please." Janet followed Audrey into the house but stopped in the doorway at the natural light that greeted her from a row of nearly floor-to-ceiling windows along the back wall. "Audrey, this is gorgeous! The light, the trees, that patio—it's all wonderful."

"It *is* a pretty view, isn't it?" Audrey led the way into the sun-drenched sitting room. "Mama would have loved all the trees."

"You can enjoy them on her behalf."

Audrey tilted her head for a moment in contemplation then carried the pie to a small two-person table optimally positioned to enjoy the view. "I guess that's one way to think about being here without her."

"It's a way to bring her into this house." Janet wandered over to a row of pictures lined up on a narrow table on the far side of the room. "You've been to Ireland and London?"

"Mama and I did a fair amount of traveling when I first retired from nursing. There were so many places we'd always talked about seeing but never had. So we remedied that."

Janet pointed at one of the photos. "Scotland too? Ian would be pleased. We're hoping to go there someday, perhaps for our fiftieth wedding anniversary."

Audrey removed the pie from the box, set out two plates, and added a pair of forks. "You said he grew up here, right?"

"Mostly, yes. His parents emigrated from Scotland when he was a young boy. Fortunately for me, he kept the brogue I love so dearly." Janet studied the picture of the Scottish countryside and the faces of its people, just visible in the background. "Ian has blue eyes, as I'm sure you've noticed, but did you know that the highest concentration of green eyes is found in Scotland, Ireland, and northern Europe?"

"I did not. Interesting that he doesn't have them." Audrey started the coffee maker on her kitchen counter.

"His father did, and so does Tiffany. So the Scottish bloodline is certainly represented. As it is in Tiffany's middle name, Arabella."

"What does it mean?" Audrey asked.

"'Given to prayer.'"

Audrey smiled. "That's a lovely middle name for a lovely young woman."

"Thank you." When Janet reached the last framed photograph, she moved to examine another series of pictures on a nearby book-shelf. "Actually, my husband would love all of these."

"Ian likes photographs?"

Janet smiled at the array of images and the stories they told, her thoughts bouncing between her conversation with Audrey and the places the woman had gone. "I thought *I* enjoyed looking at pictures and photo albums until I met Ian. But I kid you not when I say he could win a medal if it was an Olympic sport."

Audrey chuckled. "So, while the coffee is brewing, let me show you the rest of the place."

Janet followed her down a hallway, complimented her bedroom, and then stopped with her outside a second, largely unfurnished room.

"What are your plans for this room?" Janet asked.

"I don't have any." Audrey rested a hand on the doorframe, grief unmistakable on her face. "I can't get past the fact that this would be my mother's room if she were here with me."

"I understand that," Janet said. "What if you used it as an art room?"

"Why on earth would I dedicate an entire room to that?" Audrey asked in surprise.

"Because you have real talent, whether you realize it or not."

Audrey's answering laugh echoed around them. "I think my mother would roll over in her grave if she heard you say that."

"Say what?" Janet asked. "That you have talent, or that you should make time and space for it in this room?"

"Probably a little bit of both," Audrey said, still laughing. "Don't get me wrong. Mama was kind and loving. Larry and I were lucky to have been raised by her. She never said my drawings were bad, but when I'd show them to her when I was growing up, her smile would always change into one that seemed forced. Then she'd close her eyes for a few moments, breathing in and out slowly. When she opened her eyes again, she'd set my picture on the table or the chair or whatever was nearby and send me out to do something else. So that's what I did. Other things."

"Once you were an adult, did you ever ask her about that?" Janet asked.

"I thought about it on occasion. But I was afraid she'd take it as me critiquing the job she'd done raising me, and that was the last thing I wanted to do. So I told myself that it was a generational thing. Practicality was everything, and she didn't want to encourage me in something she didn't see as practical. In her own way, she was protecting me."

"I can see that," Janet said.

Audrey stepped into the room and directed Janet's attention past the pair of moving boxes to a lone piece of furniture—a long card table. Spread across it was the series of drawings Janet and Tiffany had found. "Yet now that these have been uncovered, there's a part of me that wonders whether it wasn't drawing in general she didn't like but rather my drawings specifically."

"Based on what I saw on that napkin the day we met, there's no way anyone could dispute your ability."

"I don't know." Audrey picked up the drawing based on the final scene of *Need It? Grow It* and studied it closely. "When you and Tiffany first gave me these drawings, I was thrown because I'd never seen them before. Mama and I shared everything with each other. Except this. But the more I've studied them, the more I've been able to consider why she had them and why she didn't say anything to me about them."

"Have you come up with anything?"

"Mama, like most farm kids, didn't have a lot of money growing up. They didn't ride on a train, or go to parties, or even go to the theater where a film like this would've been shown before a movie. People who did got their fill on the screen. But these pictures would have been a treat for Mama. Maybe one of her friends who did go to the theater saw this film and liked it enough to draw it for Mama."

It sounded unlikely to Audrey, but after all, she hadn't known Mae.

Audrey showed her the final picture. "I bet Mama was drawn to them because she kind of resembled the woman in the film at that age. And I know from conversations with her that she felt helpless during the war. Her brothers all went off to fight, and she had to stay home on the farm, which I know was hard for her. Perhaps these spoke to her because they showed her how she was helping too.

Yet, after the war, it became a painful reminder of a time that cost her so dearly, which might be why she didn't show these to me."

Janet took in the young woman, the farmhouse, the strawberry fields, and the hopeful smile of the little boy peering through the fence. "What do you mean, it cost her dearly?"

"Three of her four brothers didn't make it back from the war."

"I'm so sorry," Janet said, putting a hand on Audrey's shoulder. "My great-grandfather didn't return from the war either. I didn't know him, of course, but I knew others who did, and they missed him dreadfully."

Audrey reached up and squeezed her hand. "My mother rarely talked about that time, but from what she did say, I could tell that the ache over the death of her brothers was always with her. Eventually, though, she met my father. He too had served during the war and had even known one of my fallen uncles. After my parents married, they took over my father's family farm."

"I'm sure that was some comfort to her, to be able to connect to his heritage in that way," Janet said.

"It was," Audrey agreed. "It helped that my uncle Everett—the brother Mama had always been closest to and the one who survived the war—lived with us for the first few years of my childhood. Mama said she spent her childhood following Everett around whenever she could and that she wanted to be like him. Unfortunately, I don't remember him much beyond little flashes."

"Like what?"

"Like him in his wheelchair, staring out the window at memories Mama said he couldn't unsee. Like how Mama would bring him books to read because he'd told her since she was little that books could solve all sorts of problems, big and little. How she'd have to turn the pages of those books for him because he wouldn't so much as raise a hand to do it himself. And how, little by little, he withered away until, one day, he was gone. I remember Mama being devastated. I remember being in my bed and hearing her tell Daddy how it reminded her of the helplessness she'd felt watching Everett and the other boys go off to war while she had to stay behind. I remember the sound of her crying and knew it was a sound I never wanted to hear again."

Janet said nothing, waiting for her friend to continue in her own time.

"I think that helpless feeling she had during the war is why she wanted me to have a real job. So I could be a productive member of society in a way people could see. Myself included."

"And nursing fit that bill," Janet said, gazing at the simple yet powerful drawings again.

"It did. And it was fulfilling work, of course. But I do wish I'd been able to explore art as well somehow."

Janet pointed at the series of pictures. "I met his granddaughter last week."

"Whose granddaughter?"

"Kenneth Hartman. The man who drew *Need It? Grow It.*"

Audrey's gaze snapped to Janet's. "Really? What a treat!"

"It was. His artwork was used a lot during the war, mostly for the soldiers. But this one was different, and it was the one that truly kicked off his career."

Slowly, Audrey lowered the final drawing back to the table. "I don't know who drew these or why my mother never told me about them, but they obviously mattered to her if she kept them. I think I'm going to frame this last one and hang it here, in the room that would've been hers. A tribute to her and the productive member of society she was. As both a woman who raised the two hardworking people my brother and I grew to be, and a woman who helped feed the people in her community during a dark time in our nation's history."

Janet gave her an encouraging smile. "I think that's a lovely idea, I really do. And when you do, would you mind if I took a picture of it and sent it to Kenneth's granddaughter, Stacy? That way she can see how his work still matters today."

"Of course you can."

"I think this room with its natural light would be a lovely place for all sorts of things that can help you feel connected to her."

"What did you have in mind?" Audrey asked.

"Did your mother like to read?"

"Very much."

Janet pointed. "That corner would be perfect for a comfy reading chair. And since your mother clearly enjoyed these drawings enough to save them, you should bind the ones you don't frame into a book or something. Then you can use this table to draw your own pictures."

Audrey laughed. "You don't give up easily, do you, Janet?"

"Not on things that shouldn't be given up on. You have no reason to prioritize practicality now that you're retired."

"I'll give it some thought, I guess," Audrey said with a small smile.

"I'll hold you to that." Janet looped one arm through Audrey's. "Now let's go have some pie and coffee. Then we can get to work."

Together, they made their way back to the airy kitchen. While Janet took a seat, Audrey filled two mugs with coffee and set one at each of their spots.

"You're my first guest," Audrey said, sitting in the chair opposite Janet's.

"But not your last." Janet smiled at her.

"I must say, you being here is a nice change from the way it's been since I moved in." Audrey cut two slices of pie and slid them onto plates. "Though, if I'm honest with myself, it was that way in my old place after Mama passed. I didn't have the heart to make small talk when the grief was fresh, and then being alone became a habit."

Janet took a bite of pie and chased it down with a sip of coffee. "But that's why you came here, right? For a fresh start?"

"I thought so. But being here, in a place Mama never sat in, never laughed in, never breathed in—well, it's making me feel as if I've erased every trace of her from my life. Which is the last thing I want to do."

"What *do* you want to do?" Janet asked.

"To lessen the emptiness." Audrey paused with a bite of pie in midair and then lowered it, untouched, back to her plate. "It was everywhere in the old place. It was at the kitchen table where we always ate our meals together. It was in the living room where we competed against one another while watching our favorite game shows. It was out on the patio where we listened to the birds and laughed over the antics of two crazy squirrels that liked us as much as we liked them. And it was inside her bedroom doorway where I would stand each night and tell her I loved her."

Janet lowered her own fork, speechless.

"So what did I do?" Audrey continued. "I moved here in the hope the pain would lessen, but now the absence of all those places has brought an entirely different kind of emptiness."

Wrapping her hands around her coffee mug, Janet leaned forward. "It doesn't have to."

"She was never here," Audrey replied, staring at her mug.

"*You're* here, Audrey. And she's in your heart, always. The memories you have—of sharing meals, competing over game shows, listening to birds, and saying 'I love you'—are still there for you, because it's not the place that matters. It's the person."

"Who's gone," Audrey whispered, glancing up.

"Physically, yes. But one of the most beautiful gifts God gave us is a mind that remembers people and voices and laughter. And a heart to treasure those things with. Those gifts are both wherever you are, regardless of your surroundings."

Audrey blinked hard against tears. "You're right. I know you are. I just—I don't know what I need to make this okay."

"You need to give yourself grace during this move. And the chance to make friends. It's okay to be happy and to do things that bring you joy," Janet said. "I suspect your mother would want that for you."

Wiping at a stray tear, Audrey said, "She would. But it feels disrespectful to her memory to focus on making good ones."

"That's what you'd want for her if the roles were reversed. You have to make plenty of good memories to tell her about when you see her again."

A slow smile made its way across Audrey's face. "I will. Thank you, Janet."

The notes of "You Are My Sunshine" pulled their attention toward Janet's purse. Janet hastily retrieved her bag from its resting spot beside the sofa and grabbed her phone. "I'm sorry, Audrey, I wouldn't normally take a call while visiting like this, but it's my daughter."

"Of course, dear. I understand."

"Thank you. I'll try to make it quick." Janet answered the call and held the phone to her ear. "Hi, Tiffany, I'm with Audrey. Is everything okay?"

"Sorry, Mom. I forgot about that. Tell her hi from me."

"I will. Is everything okay?" Janet repeated.

"You tell me. The race-car experience is a no-go."

Janet groaned. "How? Why? Are you sure?"

"I stopped by the station a little while ago to say hi to Dad. I mentioned seeing a sign about racing on the internet and how it looked like such fun." Tiffany drew in a breath and then released it in Janet's ear. "He told me to tell you that driving cars at that speed is totally overrated."

"To tell *me*?" Janet echoed.

Tiffany laughed. "I think he caught on."

"And he thought the idea was 'overrated'?"

"His exact word."

"Great." Janet sighed. "So we're back to square one with less than two weeks left."

"Mom, it'll be okay. There are more ideas on the list I made last night. Maybe one of those will be the one."

"We're talking about your dad here," Janet grumbled. "He's impossible to buy for."

"Which is why you should bake something like he's requested every time the subject of a birthday present comes up."

"I'm not baking him a present, Tiffany. We've been through this."

"Then we'll go over the list tonight while Dad is snoozing to whatever's on TV."

"Sounds good." She glanced at Audrey, noted the empty dessert plate in front of her with satisfaction, and then returned her attention to Tiffany. "I better go. I'll see you in a little while."

"Want me to make dinner?" Tiffany asked.

Janet smiled. "That would be wonderful. Your signature tacos?"

"Yep."

"That sounds great. Thank you." After ending the call, Janet said to Audrey, "I love my husband completely. He is smart, loyal, hardworking, truthful, and kind."

Audrey leaned back against her chair with a knowing smile. "But?"

"But he is the most difficult person on the face of the earth when it comes to buying him things for Christmas or his birthday."

"You still haven't figured out what to get him?"

Janet retrieved her fork and dug it into her waiting slice of pie. "Not a clue."

"And you said he has no hobbies, right?" Audrey asked.

"Good memory."

"A sport he enjoys?"

"Not really."

"But he's European. Isn't an interest in soccer supposed to be in his blood?" Audrey joked. "Do you think he'd like to learn a sport?"

Janet took another bite of pie. After she swallowed, she said, "Debbie suggested that to me, and so I tried to feel him out by taking him to the driving range after work last Friday."

"And?"

"He caught me," Janet said, forking up a piece of the crust. "And then took me out for ice cream instead."

Audrey's lips twitched in amusement across the brim of her mug. "How about an experience of some sort?"

"Tiffany found a place that would let him drive a race car around a track. But when she made mention of it in a roundabout way, he told her to tell me that driving fast is overrated." Janet wrinkled her nose. "He's blaming me for stuff I didn't even come up with now."

The twitch turned into a room-filling laugh her hostess tried and failed to squelch. "And his party is a week from Friday?"

Janet nodded, chewing.

"Didn't you tell me that he wants you to bake him something?" Audrey asked.

"He did. Does." Janet chased the last few crumbs around her plate with her index finger. "Which, as I'm sure you can imagine, I do all the time. It doesn't feel special."

"But if it's what he likes—"

"I'm making his cake, naturally. But I really want to give him something he'll never forget," Janet said. "A real present."

"What else does he enjoy?" Audrey asked.

"Life with me, apparently."

Audrey set down her mug. "Smart man."

"Says someone who is not trying to find him the perfect birthday present," Janet said.

"True."

Janet stacked her plate with Audrey's then pushed back in her chair. "Anyway, that's enough of that. I'm here to help you go through your mom's boxes, so let's get to it."

CHAPTER SIXTEEN

They weren't far into the first box of Mae Barker's personal items when Janet began to feel a sense of connection that was every bit as real as it was unexpected. Audrey's obvious love for her mother had already given her an image of someone sweet and kind, but going through the woman's prized possessions took it to a whole new level—one that had Janet's attention darting between whatever was in her hand at any given moment and a comparable item her mind's eye pulled from her own life's treasures.

"Is this you?" Janet held out a black-and-white photograph that was worn and tattered around the edges. "With your parents and brother?"

Audrey looked across the box positioned between them on the coffee table and smiled. "It is. I was three, and Larry was five. My parents took us to a fair."

Janet studied the midfifties attire worn by the fairgoers in the distance, the makeshift stage in the background sandwiched between chicken and goat pens, and finally Audrey's parents. "Your mom has some sort of ribbon on the front of her dress."

"She won the blue ribbon for the baking competition that year," Audrey said proudly.

"Do you know what she baked?"

"Apple cinnamon muffins."

"I bake those too. I'd love to see her recipe, if you have it." Janet took in Mae's no-fuss haircut and simple dress. "Did she like baking?"

Audrey tilted her head at Janet's question. "I don't know. Everything simply was with Mama."

"What do you mean by that?" Janet asked.

"Mama did everything without saying whether she liked it or not. She baked. She gardened. She cleaned. She supported my father in whatever he did. And she took care of my brother and me—making sure we did our schoolwork and our chores and said our prayers each night." Audrey reached into the box but stopped short of actually pulling something out. "I guess the best way to describe it is that she believed in practicing what she preached."

"A good way to be," Janet murmured.

"In most cases, perhaps." Audrey pulled a tan book from the box and clutched it to her chest.

"Not all?" Janet asked.

"I wish she'd had something special for herself. A hobby, a place, something."

Janet laughed. "She was hard to buy for too, huh?"

"Actually, she loved everything I got her."

"Lucky you."

"Mama focused everything on us and practical pursuits. To her, anything else was frivolous and would lead to disappointment and heartache."

Janet studied the twentysomething Mae in the picture, trying to make out the emotions on her face. "Do you think you would have pursued art if she hadn't been that way?"

"I'm not talking about me when I say that." Audrey lowered the book to her lap and reverently ran her fingers across its cover. "I'm talking about her. She was good at so many things, but she'd always push them aside for things that had to be done. For me. For my brother. For my father. For everything and everyone except herself."

"What kind of things?" Janet asked.

Audrey opened the book and flipped to the first page, every line from top to bottom filled with penciled words. "Listen to this. 'I stand at the window and look out, the fruits of my husband's labor stretching as far as my eye can see. In the spring, the promise of life peeks from the earth in varying shades of green, teasing me with what's to come. In the summer, I look upon a sea of blueberries and strawberries that will nourish hundreds, and if I'm quick, top a bowl of his favorite homemade ice cream.'"

Janet pressed her hand against her stomach. "Yum."

"Mama could word things in a way that had you listening with more than your ears."

"Do you think she wanted to be a writer if she wrote stuff like that?"

"I don't know. She wouldn't have told me even if she did. But I'm sure she would have been a good one if she'd tried."

"That book must mean a great deal to you."

Audrey's eyes grew misty. "She read poems and short stories out of it to Larry and me all the time when we were little. We loved it. But we never knew she'd written them herself until Daddy said something about it one day. She brushed it off when he did, but I don't think she ever read from it again. This is the first I've seen it since then."

"She must've been good at baking as well, to get a blue ribbon at this fair." Janet added the photo to the pile on her right.

"Mama won it every year throughout my childhood."

"Impressive."

"It was. But she saw it as a way to help my father. She wasn't after personal glory of any kind."

"How did it help?" Janet asked.

"First prize was more than a ribbon. If the grocery store sponsored the contest, she won a bag of flour or a bar of soap. If the hardware store sponsored it, she might get a box of nails or a bag of seed. And every little bit helped." Audrey flipped through a few more pages in the book and then set it down. "It was the practicality of the contest that made her enter. If not for that, she would never have done so."

Janet looked into the box, pointed out a stack of photos she suspected Audrey would enjoy going through, and then reached past them for another book. "Anything else she was good at?"

"Besides being a wife and mother? Everything, as far as I'm concerned." Audrey took the stack of photographs, thumbed through the first few, and held them out to Janet. "She took these."

Setting the book on her lap, Janet took the stack of pictures and slowly made her way through them, the lack of color taking nothing away from the beauty she found in each one.

A cow gazed at her across the rail of a fence.

The sun rose behind a field of corn.

Baby goats frolicked around their mother.

"Wow," Janet murmured. "These are really good."

"She took the first one because Daddy was selling that cow, the second because he was talking to a new market about his corn, and the next because they wanted people in town to know we had goats for sale."

Janet handed back the pictures. "Practicality struck again, huh?"

"It did. As it always did." Audrey continued through the stack until she reached the last one. "I think practicality was a cornerstone of the women from that generation, and they passed it on as the cornerstone of my generation as well. What they went through shaped them as people and as parents, which meant that it shaped us too."

"Not everyone born in your generation became a nurse or a teacher," Janet said. "My mom loved books as a child, and she went on to be an editor for a Christian publisher. And one of my friends from college had a mom who owned a bakery."

Audrey showed Janet a bracelet from the box, which she identified as having belonged to Mae's mother. "What about your friend, Debbie? What did her mother do?"

"She raised Debbie. Afterward she went to work as a receptionist for a clinic. She still works there part-time."

"Receptionist—another acceptable position for women of that time." Audrey slipped the bracelet onto her wrist, turned it this way and that way in the light, and then took it off and set it next to the pictures. "Now don't get me wrong. I loved nursing, and I was good at it. But seeing what your generation has done, and all the opportunities and choices available to your daughter's generation is exciting and a little enviable."

Janet opened the book in her lap and drew in a breath at the perfectly detailed mouse gazing at a piece of cheese from its perch on top of a booklined shelf. She drank in its long tail wrapped around the spine of the nearest book, the hopeful glint in its rounded eyes, and the unsupervised piece of cheese on a forgotten plate.

"I don't know how you've done it, Audrey, but you've made it so I'm actually rooting for the mouse to get that piece of cheese," Janet gushed. "He's adorable."

"Mouse?"

Janet rotated the book so that Audrey could see the drawing. "That expression. Those eyes. That face. He's utterly precious, and you're amazing!"

"Me?" Audrey drew back from her then leaned forward to peer at the art. "Why?"

"You drew this, didn't you?" Janet asked.

"I most certainly did not."

Returning the open book to her lap, Janet flipped through the next few pages to find the same mouse using the books to create a path to the cheese as Audrey moved to watch over her shoulder. On one of the exposed spines, Janet spied a faint *E* and an even fainter *W* above the date *November 1944*. On another, she picked out the title of one of Agatha Christie's earliest novels.

"Clever little mouse," Janet murmured.

The mouse scurried across the books as a door in the background opened. Janet flipped the page and laughed as she found the mouse frozen beside the final book as if he were a bookend. When the door closed again, she and Audrey let out a collective sigh of relief then cheered as the mouse indulged in his first piece of cheese.

She handed the book to Audrey and followed along again, picture by picture. After the third viewing, Audrey flipped through a handful of empty pages to the book's back cover.

"If not you, then who *did* draw it?" Janet prodded.

"I wish I could answer that, but I've never seen it before."

"It might have belonged to one of your uncles," Janet suggested.

For a long minute, Audrey didn't reply. Janet was about to pose the question again in case her friend hadn't heard it, but Audrey closed the book. "I suppose it's possible. Or perhaps someone sent it to Everett after the war."

"If so, I hope it made him smile the way it did us."

Audrey set the book down next to the bracelet and the pictures. "I don't remember him ever smiling, but if it did, it would explain why Mama saved it. She loved him so."

Janet reached back into the box and extracted a large envelope. She flipped it right side up and traced her fingers along the outer edges of all four three-cent stamps and then across the California postmark dated 1943. Scrawled across the center of the envelope was the name Mae Wyatt. "Wyatt was your mother's maiden name?" she asked.

"It was. How did you—oh, I see." Audrey peered at the envelope. "And that's the address where she lived with my grandparents and my uncles when she was growing up."

Janet pointed at the matching return address and then slid her finger across the envelope to the stamps. "Three cents for a stamp back then. Can you believe it?"

"No," Audrey said, laughing. "I can't."

"It feels empty, but do you want to check and see?" Janet held the envelope out to Audrey.

"I guess." Audrey took it and smiled at the writing. "Even as an early teen, as she would have been in 1943, she had such pretty penmanship."

Janet reached into the box for another stack of pictures. "Pretty penmanship has never been an attribute of mine, that's for sure."

Slowly, Audrey turned the envelope over and worked her finger under what was left of its seal. She peeked inside. "You're right. It's empty."

"Interesting." Janet looked at the first two pictures in her latest pile and then glanced over at Audrey. "I wonder why she saved it. Especially since it's not from anyone."

"Not from anyone? How could that be?"

"Look at the return address," Janet said. "It's a self-addressed envelope."

"You're right. That's odd."

"The postmark on it says California, so she probably sent away for something, and she had to include a self-addressed stamped envelope to get it," Janet suggested. "Whatever it was clearly required more than one stamp."

"Knowing Mama and what was going on in the world in 1943, it was probably something she thought would help her family."

Janet thumbed through a few more pictures and then set them on the pile for Audrey to see. "She sounds like she was a truly giving and loving person."

"The best," Audrey said, drawing the envelope to her chest. "I would love to know what she sent away for and why she thought the envelope was worth saving."

"Tiffany will probably say the same sort of thing about me when I'm gone and she's going through my things. But with me, it'll be because I put something down, and then another thing, and another thing, and suddenly things that should have been thrown in the trash are mixed together with important things. And rather than actually go through them, I toss them in a box for later sorting that never happens."

Audrey put the envelope on the coffee table. "Mama was a very particular person, and she packed these boxes herself. If she had this in with her most special possessions, there was a reason. I wish there weren't so many things I know nothing about."

Janet took another stack of photographs from the box, glanced at the top one, and held it out to Audrey. "I bet you know plenty about *this*, right?"

Audrey took the pictures, a smile spreading across her gently lined face. "This was my tenth birthday. Mama and Daddy took me to the circus."

"You all look mighty happy," Janet said.

"It was a wonderful day. I still remember bits and pieces of it as if it were yesterday. One of the clowns actually convinced Mama to be part of his act. At first she was shy, but as it went on, she got more and more comfortable. And by the time he led her back to her seat, she was smiling so big her eyes sparkled." Audrey wiped her eyes.

Janet pointed at the picture. "Clearly that day was every bit as special to her as it was to you. Focus on that. Not an empty envelope we'll probably never find out about. It's entirely possible it made its way in here by accident."

Audrey gave her a small smile. "You're right. Thank you."

"My pleasure." Janet peeked into the nearly empty box. "Just a few more photographs and three more journal-type books left in this one."

"Which I can surely handle so that you can get home to your family."

"We're fine. It's only—" Janet glanced down at her watch and gasped. "It's six thirty? I had no idea."

Audrey braced herself on the edge of the nearby sofa and stood. "I don't want you to miss your daughter's tacos."

"But we haven't even gotten into the second box yet," Janet protested. "And I'm enjoying this."

"Really?" Audrey asked, her left eyebrow arching.

"You bet. I love learning about your mother's history and, by extension, yours."

"Then we can go through the other box another day."

Janet considered that option, a smile forming on her lips as she pulled out the three remaining journals. "Which would give me another excuse to bring you pie."

"I won't argue with that. But let's stop for now. You've done enough."

"I have an aversion to leaving a job unfinished, but this is your project. Let me get these last few stray pictures out and—"

A paper sticking out from beneath a flap at the bottom of the box caught her attention. Gently, Janet lifted the strip of cardboard to reveal a typewritten letter on paper yellowed with time. "Found something else."

"What is it?" Audrey asked.

"Looks like a very old letter." Janet held the aged paper up for Audrey to take.

"It's to my mom," Audrey said, carrying it over to the lamp.

Janet took advantage of the silence that came from Audrey reading to remove the last stack of pictures and set them on the table with the others.

"This doesn't make any sense."

Janet began breaking the empty box down. "What is it?"

"It's a rejection letter," Audrey said.

"For what?"

"For a contest my mother entered."

"A baking contest?" Janet flattened the box so she could slide it into the recycling bin she'd passed at the entrance to Audrey's community.

"No."

"Photography?"

"No."

She racked her brain for the other things Audrey had said her mother was gifted in.

"A *drawing* contest." Audrey's voice sounded strained.

Janet stopped folding and stared at her friend. "But you said your mother didn't like drawing."

"I don't understand this," Audrey murmured.

Janet propped the flattened cardboard against the remaining box and then motioned for the letter in Audrey's trembling hands. "May I?"

Audrey passed it over, her face tight with confusion.

Stepping closer to the lamp, Janet held the yellowed paper in its light.

Dear Miss Wyatt,

We are sorry to say that your entry in our Wartime Animation contest did not make it past the preliminary round. Entries that did showed a natural eye and a potential for artistic growth.

While we appreciate you taking the time to submit your work, we found it lacking in both regards.

We wish you every success in your future life pursuits.

All my best,

Your mystery judge

"'All my best,'" Janet read out loud, circling back. "Really? After that letter?"

"None of this makes any sense to me." Audrey raked a shaky hand through her hair. "Mama was always shooing me away from whatever I was doodling on at home, or in the barn, or wherever we were that I happened to have paper and a pencil at my disposal."

"Right," Janet said.

"And now I find *this*?" Audrey tapped the letter in Janet's hand. "If she liked drawing enough to enter a contest for it, shouldn't she have understood how much I liked it? We could have even done it together instead of her always making me feel like I was wasting time."

Janet pulled out her phone, took a picture of the letter, and then slid her attention back to the first two paragraphs.

We are sorry to say that your entry in our Wartime Animation contest did not make it past the preliminary round. Entries that did showed a natural eye and a potential for artistic growth.

While we appreciate you taking the time to submit your work, we found it lacking in both regards.

Janet blew out a frustrated breath. "This letter is unnecessarily harsh, especially to a teenager. I can't fathom that. Can you?"

As if pulled from a trance, Audrey's gaze snapped back to Janet's. "Can I what?"

"Imagine sending a letter like this to a young person." Janet shook the letter. "No wonder her interest soured the way it did."

"Her interest?"

"In drawing. For herself for obvious reasons. But for you too. No loving parent would ever want their child to be hurt like this. I bet she couldn't stand the idea of someone writing a letter like this to you."

Audrey reclaimed the letter and read it again, silently. When she reached the bottom, she sighed. "Of course."

"I would never want words like that to be written or said to Tiffany about something she enjoyed," Janet continued. "Because, right or wrong, it's the hurtful things we tend to remember most, especially when we're young and trying to find our way."

"This all makes sense now," Audrey murmured. "So much sense."

Janet retrieved the folded box. "I think we have to consider the possibility that your mother actually did draw those pictures Tiffany and I found."

"No. That's not possible."

"But we know she used to draw."

Audrey shook her head. "Clearly not well enough to draw things like *that*."

"Maybe she kept at it and improved." Janet held up her finger, crossed to her phone, and opened her search engine. She typed in her question and pressed enter. "*Need It? Grow It* came out at the beginning of 1944. Perhaps she'd gotten better by then, enough to recreate the art."

"Mama was the lone child on the farm in 1944. There wouldn't have been time to go to a movie, let alone work up to the level of those drawings from a place that had earned her this kind of response." Audrey looked back down at the letter, her lips moving silently as she read it to herself once again. "It must have been a friend. Someone who thought the film reminded her of Mama and what she was doing to help the war effort."

"I guess," Janet said, but she wasn't sure at all.

"She wanted to draw," Audrey murmured. "She tried. She wasn't good at it."

Janet glanced back at her friend, unable to read her expression. "But *you* are, Audrey. You were directed away from it. Quite likely because of that letter rather than because of your actual work."

"I pursued what I was meant to pursue." Audrey blew out a long, slow breath. "Though this letter answers a question—something I've revisited often the past two years."

"What's that?"

"A few years before Mama passed, I bought a little box of conversation starters that I found in a gift shop while we were traveling. I thought it would be a fun way to spice up our dinners once we got back home, and it did. But one day, the question we pulled out was about childhood dreams. I said mine had been to be an artist. She got this funny expression that I assumed, based on everything she'd ever said on the subject, would be followed with something about reality and worthwhile pursuits, but she didn't say anything. At all."

"Did you ask the same question of her?" Janet asked, intrigued.

"I did," Audrey replied. "She didn't say anything. She just squeezed my hand."

"How odd," Janet said.

"At the time, I thought that squeeze was her letting me know that having a family like ours had been her dream. But now, in light of this letter, I have to wonder if she was actually feeling the same way I was. Because her childhood dream may well have been the same as mine. I understand why she didn't tell me. She would rather have me focus on a career where I wouldn't be hurt the way she was. But I feel like I missed out on a huge part of who she was because I didn't know about this."

Tucking the box under one arm, Janet encircled Audrey's shoulders with the other. "I think that makes a lot of sense."

"I still wish I'd known about this letter," Audrey said.

"Why? What could you have done?"

"I could have reminded her that this was one person's opinion. That's all."

"And a not a very nice person, at that," Janet said, stepping away. "And from what I've heard, every creative person faces rejection at some point. It's part of the deal. It means your work wasn't right for that situation, not that it's no good."

Audrey lifted her chin. "I'd give anything to be able to tell her that."

"I'm going to head home." Janet hefted the flattened box. "I'll put this in the recycling bin on my way out of your neighborhood."

"Thank you, Janet."

"Anything else I can drop in there for you since I'm stopping anyway?"

Audrey held up the letter. "How about this?"

"Not a chance. A recycling bin is *far* too good for that letter, as far as I'm concerned." Janet crossed into the kitchen and retrieved her bag. "I think we should take it to that community firepit you mentioned earlier and burn it. With or without s'mores. That judge's cruel words should never be seen again."

"Burn it," Audrey repeated softly. A smile broke over her face. "I like the sound of that. A lot."

Janet smiled. "I'll bring matches next time."

CHAPTER SEVENTEEN

ot a single guess on even one puzzle?"

Startled away from the game show she hadn't been watching, Janet paused her hand on Ranger's back and mustered a smile for her husband. "Tonight's contestants are on the ball."

Ian's eyes narrowed on Janet. "I'm not buying that. There's always at least one contestant on the ball every time we watch this, and you still yell out the answer before they do."

"Be careful. You might inflate my ego."

"When it comes to this show, you've earned the right to an inflated ego. I'm convinced you could win the whole thing if you actually went on it."

Janet shrugged.

"Okay, okay." Ian shut off the TV and closed his favorite recliner with a resounding thud. "The busy-day excuse isn't working for me anymore."

Before she could pat Ranger back into the deep slumber he'd been enjoying, Ian crossed to the couch, transferred the cat to the open spot beside Laddie, and sat down beside her. "You haven't been yourself since you got home this evening. And this on a night where Tiffany took care of dinner and cleanup."

Janet shot up straight on the couch. "Oh no. Did I forget to thank her for the tacos?"

"No, you thanked her. It sounded rather automated, but you did it." Ian slid his arm around Janet's shoulders and gently guided her back against the couch. "But she and I did most of the talking during the meal, and you've been silent since we came in here to watch your show. It's not like you."

Janet rested her cheek against his shoulder. "I'm just tired."

"Nope. Tired Janet yawns and has us watch TV without the lights on. *Really* tired Janet puts her feet on the coffee table while she watches whatever show is on and possibly drifts off." Ian tapped her nose. "This Janet hasn't yawned once. The lamp is still on. And your feet are firmly on the floor. You're radiating energy, which makes me think you won't sleep much better tonight than you have the last several nights."

"I had no idea I was such a transparent person," she joked.

"After twenty-plus years of evenings together, I know what's normal and what's not. I'm highly observant and sensitive, you see."

She gave up. Ian would only tolerate so much secrecy, and it seemed she'd found that limit. "I had a friend in high school who wanted to be a writer. She put all her time into that dream. She wrote for the school paper, worked on the yearbook, wrote short stories for fun—anything and everything you can think of. She was always talking about going to college and majoring in journalism."

"Okay." It was clear from her husband's tone that whatever he'd expected her to say, that wasn't it.

"And then one day she stopped," Janet said. "She quit the paper and the yearbook, and no longer carried a notebook around the way she always had."

"Do you know why?" Ian asked.

"I didn't at the time. I assumed that something else caught her fancy. But a few years later, I ran into her at a party. I asked her the usual question about what she was majoring in. I was shocked when she said she wasn't even going to college. That she couldn't justify the tuition when she had nothing she wanted to do or be."

"That's odd," Ian said.

"I asked about her writing and what happened to it." Janet set her hand on Laddie's back. "She gave it up because during our junior year of high school, an English teacher told her she wasn't any good at it."

"A *teacher* said that?" Ian asked, his eyes wide.

"Yes, a teacher." Janet moved her hand to the top of Laddie's head and played with the dog's ear. "And because of his unkind words, this girl not only gave up a career, she lost faith in herself altogether. She could have done any number of other things, but he extinguished her spark."

Ian rested his cheek on the top of Janet's head. "People like that shouldn't teach."

"Agreed. Unfortunately, they sometimes do, and they end up passing on terrible, untrue lessons."

They sat that way for a few moments until, finally, Ian planted a kiss on her hair and lifted his head. "Thank you for telling me why you've been so quiet. What brought that memory and the following thought process to your mind tonight?"

"Audrey's mother entered a drawing contest in her teens. It was for animation." Janet straightened and twisted toward him. "We found the rejection letter she got while going through some of her things after work this afternoon."

Ian searched her face closely. "And?"

"It was cold and unnecessarily harsh. It was cruel, quite frankly. I don't understand why the judge felt it was appropriate to respond that way. He or she could have simply said, 'Thanks for submitting your work, but unfortunately we were not able to move forward with your entry. Please try again in the future.' Something kind and encouraging that still relayed the message. But it was as if the judge wanted to break her spirit."

"That's why it got you thinking about your high school friend," Ian said.

"It was awful, Ian. Truly. I wasn't even the recipient, but it broke my heart. I can't imagine how Audrey feels, seeing how someone once wrote to her mother and destroyed her faith in herself."

Ian took her hand. "I'm sorry to hear that, my love. It's hard to understand people like that. But as Pastor Nick says, those are the people we need to pray for."

"They make it hard," Janet grumbled.

He laced his fingers between hers and squeezed. "They do indeed."

"The worst part about that is how its damaging message affected two lives."

"You mean the teacher's words for your friend and the rejection letter for Audrey's mother?" Ian asked.

"I'm talking specifically about the rejection letter now."

He frowned in confusion. "I'm not following."

"Mae was around thirteen when she entered that contest, based on the date. It appears the cruelty of that rejection letter may have played a hand in making her give up on something she wanted."

"Mae is Audrey's mom, right?"

"Right. And if that isn't sad enough all on its own, that same rejection letter is very likely why Audrey herself has done nothing with her own talent for drawing."

"How so?"

"Mae directed Audrey away from art by pushing more practical pursuits—something Audrey attributed to her mother's pragmatic generation. But since we found that letter, I'm not so sure anymore. What if Mae's discouragement was primarily about protecting her daughter from the kind of hurt she'd suffered?"

"That would be unfortunate."

"It would be," Janet agreed. "Because from what I saw of Audrey's drawing ability the day I met her, she is incredibly talented."

Ian rubbed his jawline. "You showed me the napkin she drew on when you got home that night. And, yeah, there's some serious talent there."

"Yet one letter from one 'mystery judge' may have been why she never got to see where that talent could take her."

Ian squeezed her hand. "You can't go back and change it. All you can do is encourage her whenever you happen to see something she draws."

"I've only seen the one thing," Janet said. "I definitely want to keep supporting her as much as I can."

"Mom?"

Janet caught sight of her daughter peeking around the hallway corner with her tablet held against her chest. "Yes, Tiffany?"

"Can we talk for a minute?"

"Of course. Come sit." Janet started to pat the sofa cushion but stopped when her hand came down on two coats of fur. "Oops, sorry, guys. I almost forgot you were there."

"Don't move them. We can sit in my room instead," Tiffany said.

"We could sit in the kitchen," Janet said, rising from the couch. "I brought cookies home."

Tiffany shook her head. "Really, Mom, my room would be better."

Janet started to protest, but Ian cut her off. "Our daughter wants to talk to you, Janet. Without me around."

"No she doesn't. She…" The rest of Janet's sentence faded away as she locked eyes with her nodding daughter. "Oh. Right."

Tiffany's eye roll earned another laugh from Ian. "Go on," he said as he shifted into the place vacated by Janet's departure. "Enjoy your girl time. I'll be right here with Laddie and Ranger when you get done." He sank back into the cushions, obviously preparing for a nap.

Janet chuckled. "I know enough to let sleeping dogs—plus cats and husbands—lie. Enjoy your nap."

Tiffany led the way down the hallway to her room, muttering something inaudible beneath her breath until they were safely out of Ian's earshot. "Mom, I'm doing my best with this surprise for Dad. Help me out a little."

"Sorry about that." Janet joined Tiffany on her bed. "But I'm here now, so what's up?"

Tiffany crisscrossed her legs and held out the tablet. "I found another possibility you might want to consider for Dad's gift." She rotated the screen as a picture of a chef's hat and rolling pin came up.

Janet scrolled down the page, registering a floured countertop, a mixing bowl surrounded by baking staples, a pair of cupcake tins filled with batter, and a plate of frosted treats.

"I think your dad would prefer cheesecake or brownies to cupcakes." She dismissed the idea with a flick of her hand. "But it doesn't matter. I told you, I bake for him all the time. That's not a good enough birthday present."

"But taking a class where Dad can learn how to bake might be. It combines the idea for an experience rather than a material gift with his love of baked goods."

"A baking class?" Janet stared at her daughter.

"Definitely. Dad could get a little taste of what you do, understand the process of it all a little more, and then eat his own efforts at the end of the class. Which you could do with him if you wanted, since you're another of his favorite things. Even if he doesn't take up baking as a hobby, he'll at least have a greater appreciation for your skill."

Janet gazed at the plate of frosted cupcakes on the screen. "If someone is going to teach Dad how to bake, it'll be me. And I'd do it with some of his favorite recipes."

"Then do it," Tiffany said. "I actually like that idea even more, and Dad would too. He loves spending time with you, Mom. And he loves eating the stuff you bake. This would combine the two."

"Me teaching Dad how to bake isn't a present, Tiffany. It's something I could do with him any old time."

"But you haven't."

"Because he wants to eat what I make, not make it himself," Janet said.

"Have you ever asked him if he'd like to learn?"

She considered her daughter's question, but the answer came quickly. "No."

"So get him a class." Tiffany swept Janet's attention back to the screen. "Or, better yet, give him one of your own, which, like I said, I think he'd enjoy even more. You could have a ton of fun with it."

"I'll give it some thought." Janet slid off the bed. "For now, though, how about some cookies that are already made? I have oatmeal scotchies with extra butterscotch chips. You love those."

"How could I say no to that?" Tiffany said, laughing.

Janet laughed with her, but then her attention was caught by the latest addition to the bulletin board that hung above Tiffany's desk.

"You kept the napkin?" Janet asked. "The one Audrey sketched on?"

Tiffany got off the bed. "I had to."

"Why?"

"It's one of my newest dreams to live in a house like that one day. It's a perfect addition to my vision board. One of my teachers told us that visualizing goals this way helps you achieve them."

Stepping closer to the penciled sketch on a Whistle Stop Café napkin, Janet took in the cheerful cottage with its clapboard siding, brick accents, arched windows, flower-flanked walkway, and pair of welcoming rockers on the front porch as her daughter's words took root in her thoughts. "Your newest dream, huh?"

"I know, I know. I have a lot of dreams, but they're all things I want to do, places I want to go, and stuff I want to try in my lifetime," Tiffany explained. "But don't worry, they're not all for right now or even the next few years. They're all dreams for different stages in my life, which is why I like them so much."

"Take me through them," Janet said.

"Okay. I'd like to land a job right after college then take a few fun trips here in the States with my friends. Then meet a good man sometime after that and get married at our church. I want to make you a grandma at least twice and take my children on amazing vacations like you and Dad did with me. And then, when my kids are grown and on their own, I'll travel internationally with my husband. Especially to Scotland, so I can show him where Dad came from."

"That sounds marvelous. And where does Audrey's cottage fit in?" Janet asked.

"It's where we'll live when we're married and have at least our first child. Like when I'm thirty or thirty-five."

One by one, Janet admired the pictures or memorabilia pinned to the bulletin board, each a nod to one of the dreams Tiffany had mentioned. A college diploma and photos of the Pacific coastline and Grand Teton National Park. The young man holding a bouquet of flowers, and the bridal dress. The two children, in matching colors, playing in a sandbox together. The castle at a theme park and the airplane over Scotland.

And tacked in the center of them all was the Whistle Stop napkin of Audrey's sketch.

"They're all dreams for different stages in my life," her daughter had said. She'd been absolutely right.

Again, Janet took in the dreams Tiffany had chosen to showcase and thought about the life stage her daughter had envisioned for each. When she landed on the last one, she slid her focus back to Tiffany.

"So, your last one is to travel internationally?" she asked.

"It's one of my later ones, for after the other ones happen. But I can't say it's my last." Tiffany rocked back on her heels and smiled. "I don't want there to *ever* be a time in my life when I'm not still reaching for some sort of dream. Even if it's only to beat my husband in a wheelchair race in whatever nursing home we wind up in."

Janet smiled at the playful image her daughter's words evoked. "My money's on you, my dear. Always."

"Thanks, Mom." Tiffany wandered back to her bed and sat on the edge. "I know opening the café last year was a big dream for you, but you still have more, don't you?"

Janet leaned her hip against the desk. "My biggest dreams in life have already come true. A great college experience, meeting and marrying your father, having you, my parents being alive and well to see all of those things happen, and yes, opening a restaurant of my own with my best friend."

"And?" Tiffany prodded.

"And what? They've all come true, thanks to God."

Tiffany gestured to the bulletin board. "You need more."

"No, I really don't," Janet said. "I'm forty-four."

"I don't care if you're ninety-four. You're never too old to dream."

Janet's gaze landed on Audrey's sketch again. Yes, Audrey was in her seventies. Yes, she had worked a long, successful, and admirable career as a nurse.

But she had real, honest-to-goodness talent.

"Audrey had a dream when she was your age," Janet said, turning back to her daughter. "She wanted to be an artist. Unfortunately, she couldn't pursue it at the time."

"There's no reason she can't go after it now, is there?" Tiffany asked. "I mean, if she can still draw like *that*, who cares how old she is?"

The questions ignited a deep and unwavering conviction. "You're right. No one cares about age when it comes to drawing, except perhaps Audrey herself. Fortunately, this conversation has shown me that I need to convince *her* not to care either."

Tiffany gently guided Janet toward her bedroom door and, beyond that, the promised cookies. "You can do it, Mom. I know you can."

"From your mouth to God's ears," Janet replied.

CHAPTER EIGHTEEN

*J*anet scanned every nook and cranny in the kitchen, her hands planted on her hips.

"Was I imagining it, or was today super busy?" she asked, glancing over at her business partner. "I feel like this is the first time I've stood still since I walked in here this morning."

Debbie's smile widened. "I'll know more later, when I crunch the numbers, but it might have been our busiest Tuesday yet."

"My neck thinks it was." Reaching for her shoulder, Janet worked at a knot with tired fingers. "But what a great problem to have, right?"

"Right." Debbie wandered to a plate of leftover brownies. "My favorite part, though, is in those brief moments when there's a lull at the register and I hear the happy chatter between friends and strangers. Knowing we created a space like that feels good, you know?"

Janet slipped off her apron and hung it on the hook to her left. "I do. And I think about that a lot. How my love of baking and your business experience brought us the café and how the people who come here have turned it into what it is—a place to gather and enjoy each other's company."

"God is good."

"God *is* good," Janet repeated. Then she yawned. "Goodness. I think I'm more tired than I realized."

Lifting her hands, Debbie shooed Janet toward the door. "Go sit down. I'll bring us both coffee and brownies so we can hammer out the final details for Ian's party next week."

"I am not ready for that at all." Janet dropped her head into her hands and groaned.

"Knowing you the way I do, I doubt that. But we'll take care of any loose ends now." Again, Debbie shooed Janet in the direction of the dining area. "So scoot."

Janet held up her hands in surrender and made a beeline for the opposite side of the kitchen. "Okay, okay, I'm scooting."

"Yes, but in the wrong direction," Debbie said, pointing toward the door. "The dining area is *that* way."

"I know." Janet stopped at the counter closest to the café's exterior door and scooped up a pile containing a notebook, a few magazines, and the to-do list she'd managed to make while brushing her teeth and combing her hair before work that morning. "We need *this* to prep for the party."

"That's a lot of stuff for one birthday party."

"I want it to be special," Janet said, hurrying past her friend once more. "Ian deserves it."

Out in the dining area, she crossed to the room's biggest table and arranged the contents of the pile across its surface. She opened each magazine to the page that had caught her eye as Debbie approached.

"Would you sit? Please?" Debbie paused so Janet could grab the brownie plate from the crook of her arm, and then set two mugs of coffee on the table. "Not more than five minutes ago you were ready to drop from exhaustion and now"—she motioned toward the sea of color in front of them—"you're a flurry of activity."

"There's a lot to do and only ten days left in which to do it." Janet dropped onto her chair and took a quick gulp of the strong coffee. "Can you believe how fast it came?"

Debbie selected a brownie. "You already planned the menu. You know who's coming. You've chosen the music. The personalized Scottish tea bags you ordered as favors arrived on Friday. Tiffany is working on the slideshow. So what could possibly be left that requires more time than we have?"

Swapping her coffee mug for a pen, Janet added a check next to *Party Favors* and circled Tiffany's name beside *Slideshow*. She scooted the brownie plate off an open magazine and pointed at the colors lined up across the page. "I haven't settled on a color for the party yet. One minute I'm leaning toward his favorite color, blue, and the next I'm leaning toward green, like the Scottish countryside."

"Do two colors," Debbie suggested between bites.

Janet stared at her friend. "Really?"

"You could, but I'm thinking more about an overall nod to Ian *and* his heritage."

"Go on," Janet said, leaning forward.

"The Scottish flag is blue and white, right? So go with those colors. That way you're acknowledging both at the same time."

"Blue and white." Janet gazed around the café. "I could use those colors with the balloons and the streamers."

Debbie licked her fingers. "Also, if you got tablecloths in that same blue, you could make an *X* across them with white streamers to look like the Scottish flag."

Janet visualized her friend's suggestion. "That's sensational."

"Perfect. Now you can check that one off too." Debbie pointed Janet back to her to-do list. "See? It'll all get done."

Janet scribbled a note of the colors next to *Decorations*. "I still need to buy it all, but yes, at least there's a plan now."

"So, what's left?" Debbie asked, craning her neck for a better view of Janet's list. "Everything is either checked or circled."

"Everything except the first, and arguably the most important, one." Janet pointed at *Ian's Gift* on the top line.

"It's underlined."

"It's underlined because it still needs to be done."

"Okay, but why is it underlined five times?"

Janet sighed and added a sixth. "Because I still can't figure out what to get him."

"I'm sorry Greg's golf lesson idea didn't work out."

The quick yet unmistakable smile that crossed Debbie's face at the mere mention of Greg lifted Janet's spirits a little. "It was still a good idea, and I made sure to thank him when I was leaving the café to go to Audrey's house after work yesterday. He was right outside the depot when I saw him. Did he pop in to see you after I left?"

"He did, actually. So golf isn't Ian's thing. That's fine. Try something else, like tennis or pickleball. You could both take lessons and then play together."

"Pickleball lessons could be fun. It certainly seems like *the* thing to do these days, doesn't it?" Janet helped herself to a brownie. "It feels like more of a present than the one Tiffany suggested last night."

"Oh?" Debbie asked. "What was that?"

"She thought, since her dad always says he wants me to bake him things, that I could enroll him in a baking lesson of his own or perhaps take it with him."

Debbie wrapped her hands around her mug. "I don't think they could teach him anything you couldn't teach him. And better, I might add."

"Thanks."

Debbie lifted her mug in acknowledgement and then took a sip.

"Tiffany suggested that I give Ian a class also. But teaching him how to bake isn't any more of a present than making him his favorite desserts. Because I bake him things all the time, birthday or no birthday."

"But teaching him how to do it could be fun," Debbie said.

Janet broke off a piece of brownie. "Maybe. But how would that be a present?"

"Not all presents have to be wrapped, Janet."

"I know that. I really do. But telling him things like 'Oops, you got a little eggshell in there' and 'Whoa, a bit less vanilla next time' doesn't seem like a gift. Who wants to sign up to be criticized by their wife about something they enjoy?"

"Is too much vanilla even a thing?" Debbie asked, laughing.

Janet grinned. "You'd be surprised. And the point is, I want something more present-y."

"I'm not sure that's a word."

Janet popped the last bite of her brownie into her mouth. "If it's not, it should be," she said after a moment. "Besides, you know what I mean."

"You still have time." Debbie grabbed the brownie plate and stood. "You'll come up with something stellar, I'm sure."

"You clearly have more faith in my abilities than I do."

"How could I not?" Debbie asked. "I've known you for forever."

Janet smiled up at her friend, though the smile cracked into a yawn. "A blessing I thank God for every single day, that's for sure."

"Ditto. Now, go home and give your brain a break. A person can only run on all cylinders for so long before they—wait! I've been wanting to ask you about helping Audrey yesterday, and I forgot. Let me take care of these things, and then you can fill me in."

Debbie disappeared into the kitchen while Janet gathered her planning materials. When Debbie returned, Janet filled her in on the previous afternoon and evening going through Mae's boxes as well as the discovery of the rejection letter.

"So Mae liked drawing as well?"

Janet made a face. "Or did until someone who had no business judging a contest told her she had no talent."

"How awful," Debbie said.

"Agreed."

Seconds became minutes as they each retreated into their own thoughts, Janet peppering the silence with sporadic yawns.

"Do you think the brother could be the one who drew those sketches based on Kenneth Hartman's animated short?" Debbie finally asked.

Janet hadn't considered that, but she was immediately sure of the answer. "Larry? No. Audrey told me that he liked her drawings, but he was only interested in using pencil and paper to do things with numbers."

Debbie was shaking her head before Janet had even finished speaking. "Not Audrey's brother. *Mae's* brother. The one in the wheelchair."

"Everett?" Janet frowned. "Why would you ask that? From what I understand, he returned from the war all but nonresponsive."

"I don't know. I guess because he's someone who'd been in Mae's life. Someone important in her life, from what Audrey told you."

"I hadn't really given it any thought, but you could be right," Janet said. "Though I doubt he'd have seen that film. He was serving when it came out, remember?"

"I didn't think about that. Did you find anything else of interest yesterday?"

"No. Just photographs and—wait." Janet straightened. "A journal. With a story about the antics of the sweetest mouse, told completely in pictures."

"Pictures?" Debbie echoed. "What kind of pictures?"

Janet closed her eyes to revisit the pictures of the mouse, relaying the story to Debbie as well as she could remember it. "They were done in pencil," she added. "And they were storybook worthy."

"Would you say the same about the copies of *Need It? Grow It?*"

"I would. Without a doubt. Each was heavily detailed." She paused to consider Debbie's words. "You're thinking the same person drew both, aren't you?"

"I am."

"Seeing as how they were both in Mae's things, and they were both drawn by someone with a lot of talent, it's certainly possible."

The notion that the same person had drawn both did make sense. Janet couldn't believe she hadn't thought of it herself. This was the benefit of talking things through, especially with someone as sharp as Debbie, who was likely to give her a perspective she never would have imagined.

She replayed everything she'd told Debbie in her head, silently marveling at the story about the mouse using the—

"He used books to get to the cheese," Janet said, smacking her hand on the table. "Everett loved books before the war. He told Mae they could provide the solution to everything."

Was that it?

Was *Everett* responsible for the mouse story? And for the copies of Kenneth Hartman's most popular wartime short?

If so, had he—the brother Mae had always looked up to—been the reason Mae had entered a drawing contest during the war? To make herself feel closer to him somehow? To make him proud of her? To—

"One of the books had an *E* and a *W* on the spine," she said. "I didn't think much of it at the time, but maybe that's why they were there, for Everett Wyatt. Oh, Debbie, this is good. Very, very good."

Debbie flapped a hand at her. "I simply threw out his name as a possibility. You connected the dots."

"If this is right, it brings the family connection to that first set of drawings even closer to Audrey. Because now, instead of merely being pictures a friend might've drawn for her, it was her uncle who drew them, likely for Mae."

"Do you want to call her about all of this?" Debbie asked.

"I think it would be more fun to share it with her the next time I see her."

"Agreed. In the meantime, go home and pamper yourself. Sleep. Read. Play with Laddie and Ranger. Whatever you want. You need a break."

"After Ian's party, I'll do a little self-care." Janet gathered her materials and stood in time to feel a vibration in her pocket. "This is probably Tiffany asking when I'm coming home."

"*Now*. You're going home *now*," Debbie ordered.

"Right." Janet scanned the screen, furrowed her brow at the Cleveland area code, and answered. "Hello?"

"Mrs. Shaw? This is Joe Carter—your daughter's former film history professor at Case Western."

She set the pile of birthday plans back onto the table and resumed her seat. "Dr. Carter, yes, hi. How are you?"

"Joe, please. I'm doing well, thank you."

"What can I help you with?" she asked.

"Actually, I'm calling to thank you for pointing me in the direction of your friend at the depot museum there in Dennison."

Janet smiled. "Kim Smith. I take it you two have spoken?"

"We have. In fact, I'm heading down there tomorrow to show her my collection of animated short films for a possible exhibit there this summer," he said.

"That would be wonderful for people to see, Joe."

"I agree." He paused. "Anyway, my reason for calling you is twofold—or perhaps threefold if you count my interest in getting my hands on another blueberry or raspberry scone."

Janet's chuckle earned a raised eyebrow from Debbie. "I think that can be arranged. And the other two things?"

"First, I was hoping you might have an update for me on those pictures you found based on *Need It? Grow It.*"

"Actually, I might, but I need to discuss it with someone first. I have something very cool to share with you about Kenneth Hartman himself."

"What's that?"

"I met his granddaughter, Stacy. My friend and I spent an evening with her last week for a behind-the-scenes look at his wartime career."

"Are you serious?" he asked.

"I am. It was really interesting."

"You know I want to hear more."

"I can't wait to share everything I learned and saw with you," Janet said. "It was all pretty fascinating."

"I'm sure it was."

"And the last thing you wanted to ask?"

"I'm not sure how exciting you'll find it, but I found the material I assembled on Kenneth Hartman during my own college years. I thought you might enjoy seeing some of it."

"I'd love to! Do you know what time you'll be here tomorrow?"

"My meeting with Kim Smith is at eleven o'clock. I imagine it won't go any longer than an hour. Can I stop by your café after?"

"Perfect. I'll be on the lookout for you around noon. With any luck, we'll be able to sneak in a little time to visit."

Debbie gave her a thumbs-up. They would make it work.

"Thank you, Joe," Janet said. "I'm looking forward to it." She would jump at any opportunity to find answers for Audrey.

CHAPTER NINETEEN

*J*anet had taken out the final tray of cookies and set the latest batch of bread to rise when Debbie breezed into the kitchen. "Joe Carter is here to see you, Janet."

"Gracious. He's early." Janet washed her hands. "Can you give the cookies ten minutes to cool and then put them in the display case?"

Debbie crossed to the pan and inhaled the sweet aroma. "Of course. Though, to be honest, I kind of hope only twenty-two of these twenty-four actually sell."

Janet laughed. "In need of a sugar boost?"

"In *need*? No." Debbie grinned. "In *want*? Absolutely. But it's your fault for making them so delicious."

"If they all sell, I'll make you a dozen of your own."

"I can't eat a dozen cookies by myself," she protested.

"Then share some of them." Janet untied her apron and hung it on its peg.

"With?"

"I hear that teenage boys are always hungry, and I happen to know that your friend Greg has two of those."

Debbie frowned. "As good as your cookies are, Janet, I'm thinking they'd be a little stale by the time church rolls around."

"Then don't wait until Sunday. Take some to his house after work." Janet tugged the hem of her yellow T-shirt down over the waistband of her pants. "Everyone loves cookies. Especially of the just-because variety."

Debbie tilted her head. "You're right. The boys would love it."

"Good." Janet quickly groomed the loose strands of her chin-length blond hair back into place and then set her hand on the gray swinging door. "I'm sure Joe and I won't be too long."

"No rush."

Janet stepped out into the chatter-filled dining area and quickly scanned the faces, both familiar and new, in search of Tiffany's professor. She spotted him at the high-top table closest to one of the windows and registered the briefcase beside his chair as well as the empty table on which he leaned his elbows.

Well, that wouldn't do. Who could work on an empty stomach?

She scooted back to the kitchen and hastily assembled a chicken salad sandwich, ladled the soup of the day into a cup, put it all on a tray, and then made a detour to the glass case beside the register. She plated up a slice of cheesecake and poured a glass of lemonade. When everything was ready, she carried it over to Joe's table.

"I see you found us." Janet set the food in front of the bearded professor and took the chair opposite his. "Welcome."

He recovered his surprise with a grin. "Is this how you welcome everyone to town?"

"If that someone was kind enough to give the mother of one of his former students several hours of his time the way you were, then yes, it is." Janet pointed at the glass. "I took a chance that you'd like lemonade. Personally, I love it with cheesecake."

He laughed. "I love lemonade."

"I'll be sure to send you home with a blueberry scone, but I thought you might enjoy a slice of cheesecake for dessert."

"I would." He took a bite of the sandwich and then wiped his mouth. "Delicious. I appreciate this very much."

She let him enjoy a few bites before asking, "What did you think of our World War II museum? Not bad for a small town like Dennison, right?"

"It is, indeed, not bad," he said with a smile. He took a bite of soup and followed it with a gulp of lemonade. "And for Kim's own mother to have served as stationmaster in this very building during the war makes it even more interesting, quite frankly."

"I couldn't agree more. Kim probably told you that Eileen lives at the retirement center here in town. Listening to her stories from that time is something I look forward to every time I see her. We'll have to get the two of you together soon."

He beamed. "I'd love that. Any chance we have to glean the wisdom of older generations is time well spent."

"That's so true. And Kim's own interest in that period is positively contagious. I know because I've seen it in action. I've been in the museum when people have stopped in out of obligation. They usually leave an hour or so later with a new respect for the service members and their country as a whole during that era."

"She has quite a music collection from that era as well," Dr. Carter said, scooting his empty plate to the side.

Janet leaned back in her chair. "And not only can she tell you who the artist was, why it was written, and how people responded to it, but she also genuinely loves it herself. Plays it all the time outside of the museum. I think it helps her feel connected to that generation."

Joe leaned down to grab his briefcase. "Sounds like me with my films. That common passion is why any hesitancy I was harboring about loaning out my wartime animation collection disappeared about ten minutes into my meeting with Kim."

"She'll take good care of them," Janet said.

"I have no doubt." He spun the numbers on the combination lock and laid the case on the table, unopened. "So, what did you learn about those drawings you showed me?"

Janet blew out a breath. "I'm not sure, actually."

"Meaning?"

"Meaning my friend Debbie and I have a thought about who may have drawn them."

Joe leaned forward, intrigued. "I'm all ears."

"It's all conjecture—which I haven't shared with anyone other than Debbie yet."

"I won't breathe a word to anyone else."

"We think they were drawn by a young man during the war— who served, in fact. But it's nothing more than a guess."

"An interesting one." He took a sip of his drink. "So tell me about your visit with Kenneth Hartman's granddaughter. How it came about. What you saw. Everything."

So she did. She told him about the article reporting the touring exhibit, Kim reaching out to Stacy and asking if Janet could speak with her, the room in the house dedicated to Hartman's work, the drawing desk, the original sketches and cels—all of it. As she spoke, she realized how special it was that she'd gotten to experience such an unlikely thing.

"I can only imagine what my paper could've been if I'd had the chance to see all of that in person," Joe said, sitting back in his chair. "Wow."

"Your paper?" Janet asked.

"Yes." He opened his briefcase and took out some papers. "I wrote an essay on Kenneth Hartman in college."

"I'd be happy to put in a good word for you so you could meet Stacy as well."

"Do you mean it?" he asked, eyes wide.

"Absolutely. You'd love it. She even has the award he won for *Need It? Grow It*."

"Does she have the original sketch pads and cels for all of his wartime work?" he asked.

"All except for *Need It? Grow It*. For that one, she just has the cels. The sketch pad was stolen from the studio right before he got his award."

"Stolen?" Dr. Carter echoed, his eyes narrowing. "I never came across that in my research on Hartman's films."

"Stacy said the studio chose not to make a big deal out of it. They wanted the story to be about her grandfather's achievement and the studio's support for the war effort."

"I believe you, but would you mind if I checked for myself? It's part of my academic training," he explained.

"Go ahead. It never occurred to me to verify what she said."

He pulled a phone from his back pocket and tapped at the screen. Seconds turned to minutes as he read, scrolled, and read some more. "Wow. You're right. There's nothing about it anywhere. It would have been an interesting thing to include in my classes."

"Stacy said there isn't anything more to tell about the incident. Her grandfather never wanted to talk about it," Janet said. "But she's determined to make sure his contributions to the war effort, as well as his career achievements, are not forgotten. Which is why I wouldn't be surprised if she'd agree to come in and talk to your classes about him. She could probably be persuaded to share with them some of the stuff I got to see."

"That would be great." He set his phone down. "It's awful that someone stole his sketches. Especially since he was so generous with his talent."

"What do you mean?" Janet asked.

"He encouraged others who had an interest in animation through contests and workshops."

"Right. Stacy mentioned that as well. She said he liked helping others."

"If only I'd been around then. I would have loved the opportunity for him to see my work." Joe laughed. "Then again, I love my job, so I can't complain."

She was taken by surprise. "Do you draw?"

"Do I draw? Yes. Am I any good? No. But with the help of a workshop given by someone like Kenneth Hartman or a contest sponsored by him, I might have been."

Janet grimaced. "If I were there with you, knowing what I know now, I'd recommend you go the workshop route rather than contests."

He drained his glass. "All a moot point for me now, considering the last time I even tried to draw something was more than a decade ago."

"Why is that?" she asked.

"Because eventually, my passion for the history of film eclipsed my desire to draw." He handed her the packet then closed and locked his briefcase.

"Thank you. I'm excited to read this."

"I'm excited to hear your thoughts." He scooted off the chair. "I should be heading out if I want to get in front of rush hour. Thank you for the meal, the cheesecake, the conversation, and for suggesting I speak with Kim. I can't wait to share my short film collection with the museum this summer. Maybe it'll speak to people the way it spoke to your daughter and to you."

Janet watched him go but not before loading him up with half a dozen scones. She had her own way of speaking to people, and she usually got results.

CHAPTER TWENTY

*A*ny chance there's a white chocolate mousse pastry hiding some- where in there?"

Straightening, Janet took in her handsome, uniformed husband across the top of the glass bakery case and beamed at him. "Will you still be glad you stopped by if I say no?"

"Being the recipient of that smile has made me completely forget what I even asked, so yes." Ian glanced over his shoulder, where no one stood behind him, and then leaned across the counter for a kiss. "Good day?"

"It is. But it's even better now." She backed up and pointed inside the case. "Whatever you want is on the house."

Ian laughed. "Thanks."

"I don't have any of those pastries today, but I do happen to have a red velvet cupcake or a peanut butter brownie if either of those strike your fancy."

"Yes, and yes."

Trading her view of the display case for one of her husband practically salivating on the other side of the glass, Janet laughed. "Does that mean you want both?"

"Would they both be on the house?" he teased.

She frowned at him playfully. "They shouldn't be. We have to make money somehow."

He laughed as she retrieved both the cupcake and the brownie. "You are still a business after all. But I think I should get one complimentary treat for being the chief of police and another for being your husband."

"That seems like you're stretching it to me, but I can't find fault with your logic." She motioned toward the white paper bags stacked on top of the display case. "Do you have time to eat these here, or do you have to get back to the station?"

He checked his watch. "I think I can eat one of them here if you have a few minutes to spare."

Janet bagged the brownie, handed him the cupcake, and motioned him over to the recently vacated counter she'd cleaned minutes before. "I'll take whatever time I can get, whenever I can get it."

Ian took a bite of the cupcake. "Wow. Every time I think I remember how good your baking is, I eat it again and it's even better."

"I'm glad."

"I've probably said this a million times, but I'm one very lucky guy," Ian said between bites.

Janet laughed. "I don't mind hearing it however many times you want to say it. Even if it's prompted by my baking ability."

"Trust me, my love. That's just one thing that makes me a lucky guy. One of many."

Crossing her arms in front of her Whistle Stop Café apron, Janet watched the cupcake disappear. "You could learn how to do it too, you know."

Ian wiped his empty hands with the napkin that had served as the cupcake's temporary plate and raised an eyebrow in question.

"Bake things like that," she said. "Red velvet cupcakes, peanut butter brownies, white chocolate mousse pastries." Janet tipped her chin toward the display case. "Cookies, pies. Anything that's in there, really. Because you could, you know, with a few lessons and some practice."

"*Me?*" Ian poked himself in the chest with an index finger.

"Sure."

"But why?"

"Because you like desserts. It would mean you could make whatever you want whenever you want it."

"Which you already do," he said, his brow furrowing.

"And I still would. But you could make your own in cases like today, where you were hoping for those pastries but I hadn't made them. If you could make them yourself, you could still have them." She cast about for another reason, another selling poin', unt'l she hit on the best one. "And it might be something fun for us to do together."

Ian started to speak but stopped as a knowing glint appeared in his eyes. "My mother often said that preparing food was a way of telling someone she loved them, and it was that much sweeter when the person appreciated it the way I do. I think I know what you're truly getting at with this."

"But—"

"You are the best birthday gift I could ever ask for this year and every other year, Janet. Please believe me." He leaned across the counter, kissed her one more time, and then motioned toward the door with the white paper bag. "I have to go. But unless something crazy comes up, I should be home around six. I love you."

"I love you too."

She watched him head out the door and climb into his police cruiser, and then returned his wave as he started it up. He rolled out of the parking lot, and she gazed after him, thanking God for her husband until a sensation of being watched made her glance at the corner table and—

"Audrey, hello!" Stepping around the counter, Janet made her way toward her friend. "I didn't know you were here. When did you arrive? Why didn't you say anything?" She caught sight of the sketch pad sitting open in front of Audrey and the pencil in her hand. "You're drawing?"

Audrey snorted. "In order to say yes, I'd have to do more with the pencil than take it out of my purse. Which I haven't yet. I'm here because I decided to expand my palate a little and try the apple pie today."

"And?" Janet asked, spotting the empty plate beyond the sketch pad. "Did you enjoy it?"

"It was delicious."

"I'm glad you liked it." Janet scooted onto the bench across the table from Audrey. "I don't know how I missed you being here."

Audrey set her pencil down. "You were talking to someone at a table by the window when I first got here. The next time I looked up from the empty page in my empty sketch pad, you were enjoying a little time with your husband and I didn't want to interrupt."

"Ian surprised me by stopping by. I love it when he does that."

"I could tell." Audrey poked at the edge of her sketch pad. "I like that he still has that hint of a Scottish accent in his voice even after all this time."

"I do too."

"He's certainly smitten with you."

Warmth crept into Janet's face, though the idea wasn't new to her. "As I am with him. I'm very blessed."

Audrey ran her fingers down the side of her pencil and then across the paper. "Still at a loss for what to give him for his birthday?"

Janet groaned. "Everything I've thought might be a good idea has proven otherwise."

"The baking lesson was a good one," Audrey said.

Janet stared at her. "You heard that?"

"I wasn't trying to listen in. I really wasn't," Audrey said, lifting her hands. "But apparently, any self-reflection I thought I was doing—in the interest of coming up with something to draw, you see—wasn't actually happening."

"It's okay," Janet assured her. "I didn't see the baking lesson idea going over anyway. But considering every other idea has proven to be a no-go, I figured it couldn't hurt to throw it out there and see if it floated. Which it didn't. Because my wonderful-in-every-other-way husband is the worst when it comes to giving me gift ideas."

"Maybe." Audrey dropped her hands back to her sketch pad. "Maybe not."

Janet laughed. "No matter how many times I ask, he says the same thing. He wants me to bake him a slew of his favorite things."

"What if you don't ask him?"

Janet stared at her. "What do you mean?"

"I mean, what if you apply what you know about him, what he likes and dislikes? Wouldn't that lead you to the perfect gift idea?"

Janet slumped in her chair. "I've tried that. Honest. But nothing is coming to mind."

"Hmm," Audrey murmured.

Before Janet could question the woman's response, a steady vibration from her apron pocket made her glance at the clock. It was two on the dot.

"Wow. Today went fast."

"Is it closing time?" Audrey asked.

Janet slid to her feet. "It is. But you're welcome to stay for however long it takes me to wipe down the tables and clean up the kitchen and for Debbie to finish the day's paperwork—probably a good thirty or forty minutes at least."

"If I was actually drawing something or still working on that slice of apple pie, I'd agree." Audrey tapped the center of the sketch pad, sending the pencil rolling. "But alas, I'm not."

Janet caught the pencil before it rolled off the table and held it out to Audrey. "I'm glad to see you with a sketch pad anyway."

Slowly, Audrey closed the pad and popped the pencil into her purse. "I've been doing a lot of thinking since we found that rejection letter. Like I told you, I never knew Mama had any interest in drawing. But now, after that letter, I feel like I should try to draw something for her."

"Like what?" Janet gathered Audrey's empty dishes.

Audrey glanced down at the closed sketch pad and shrugged. "I have no idea."

"You could draw the house you shared with your mom before moving to Dennison," Janet suggested. "Or one of the places the two of you traveled to together."

"Perhaps," Audrey hedged.

"I suspect you'll come up with the right thing when you're ready," Janet said. "And when you do, I want to see it, okay?"

Audrey frowned. "Why?"

"Because you're a really talented artist—one who came by it honestly, I'd say."

"Not according to that rejection letter we found," Audrey reminded her.

"One rejection letter doesn't mean your mother wasn't actually talented. But that's not what I meant. Everett was your uncle, yes?"

"Yes, but what does that have to do with anything?"

"Debbie and I think Everett might have been the one who drew that mouse story you and I found in your mother's box the other day."

"Why on earth would you think that?"

"Because of what you said," Janet said, sitting again. "About his belief that books were the solution to everything. Even a mouse in search of cheese. And his initials are on one of the book spines the mouse uses."

Audrey frowned at her, clearly trying to wrap her head around the idea.

Janet continued, "You said Mae and Everett were close. That she followed him everywhere, that she wanted to do everything he did."

"That's true," Audrey said.

"I wonder if that's why she entered that contest during the war— as a way to feel closer to him while he was gone. And if he was the artist in the family, we think it stands to reason that he drew those pictures based on *Need It? Grow It.*"

Audrey shook her head. "That's where you lost me. Everett couldn't have drawn the *Need It? Grow It* pictures. Or the mouse ones. He simply couldn't have."

"Why not?"

"You saw the date on the mouse pictures. He would have had to draw them after he came back from the war, and he couldn't have. He was wounded, and his right side was impacted. It was why he was in a wheelchair. Why Mama had to do things for him like writing letters and turning the pages of his books. There's no way he could have drawn those pictures."

Janet slumped in her seat. "I didn't realize. I'm sorry. We were trying to come up with an explanation."

Audrey patted Janet's hand. "It's okay, dear. I didn't tell you. It was a nice thought. It would have been so special if any talent you think I have came from him."

"Talent I *know* you have," Janet said, returning to her feet.

Pushing the strap of her purse up her shoulder, Audrey stood as well, the unused sketch pad tucked under her arm. "The drawing on that napkin was a silly little thing."

"A silly little thing that now hangs in the center of Tiffany's dream board."

Audrey stared at Janet. "Dream board?"

"The bulletin board where she's pinned pictures and things highlighting her goals and dreams for the future."

"Why is that doodled house on there?" Audrey asked, wrinkling her nose.

"Because it's what Tiffany wants her future home to look like." Janet set the dishes on the table and hugged Audrey. "Pretty impressive for someone who calls what she does 'just doodling,' don't you think?"

"Perhaps," Audrey replied. But there was a sparkle in her eyes that warmed Janet's heart.

Whether she solved this mystery or not, it would all be worth it if it revived Audrey's lifelong love. But as for Janet, it sounded like she was back at the drawing board.

CHAPTER TWENTY-ONE

Janet was putting the last bag of plates and streamers into the trunk of her car when her phone rang with a call from Ian. She answered it and willed herself to give nothing away regarding her whereabouts.

"On your way home?" Janet asked, checking her watch. "Because if you are, you might beat me by about twenty minutes."

"Are you still at the café?"

"No."

"At the grocery store?" he asked.

"No."

"Then I give up. Where are you?"

She studied the bags of color-coordinated paper products as if they would yield an answer that would be truthful without ruining the surprise. "I'm actually on my way to Debbie's to drop something off."

It was true. She was heading to Debbie's as soon as she got back in the car.

"But don't worry, Ian," she went on. "Tonight is a slow-cooker night, so I'll just have to set the table, and we'll be ready to eat."

"Unfortunately, you and Tiffany will have to start without me," Ian said. "Our media-relations officer is feeling under the weather, and he needs me to cover for him at a town meeting."

"We can wait," Janet said.

"Until nine or ten?"

She closed the trunk and made her way to the driver's side door. "That late?"

"Apparently, there's a lot on the itinerary this month," Ian said glumly.

"But what will you do for dinner?"

"I've got about forty-five minutes until I need to be there, so I'll grab something on the way."

Janet slid behind the steering wheel and started the engine. "I could run home and plate something up for you."

"Thank you, my love, but no. Go ahead and stop at Debbie's as you planned and then enjoy some mother-daughter time with Tiffany."

"I'll fix a plate for you to have when you get home or to take with you to work for lunch tomorrow," Janet said.

"That sounds great. Anyway, I'm going to head out and grab something now. I love you."

"Love you too."

Sighing, she ended the call, set the phone in the center cup holder, and started to shift into reverse, only to stop as her phone rang again. This time it was Tiffany.

"Hey, sweetie."

"Hi, Mom. I have good news, and I have bad news."

Janet tightened her grip on the phone. "Are you okay?"

"I am. I'm *great*, actually. Ashling's uncle is in town for the evening, and he's a scientist with a pharmaceutical company outside of Washington, DC."

Janet smiled. "Sounds like someone whose brain you might like to pick."

"Exactly. Which is why I think I should accept Ashling's invitation to eat with her and her family this evening."

"That's the bad news, I take it."

"Right. I think it would be really helpful to talk to him."

"I agree."

Tiffany's relief was audible through the phone. "I know you put the ingredients for your famous barbecue chicken in the slow cooker this morning, but this is too good an opportunity for me to pass up."

"I get it, Tiffany. You don't need to convince me. We have all summer. I can make you barbecue chicken another night."

"Thanks, Mom." She heard Tiffany's smile in her voice. "Enjoy dinner with Dad. I should be home by ten at the latest."

Janet started to say Ian wouldn't be eating dinner at home either but opted to let that detail go.

"I'll see you tonight," she said instead. "And have fun."

"I will. Love you, Mom."

"I love you too."

Again, she ended the call, then promptly dialed Debbie's number. Her friend didn't pick up. Before she could leave a voice mail, Debbie texted.

Hey. I'm actually a few steps away from Greg's front door with the cookies you suggested I bring to his boys. I'm sure it will only take a minute, but if for some reason I get held up, you know where I keep my spare key.

"Don't take just a minute," Janet said out loud. "In fact, take lots of minutes. With the boys, and, most importantly, with Greg."

Then she replied with a text of her own. I DO. THANK YOU.

She thought for a second and added, NO RUSH. PLEASE. I'LL PUT THE PLATES AND STUFF IN YOUR SPARE BEDROOM. SEE YOU TOMORROW.

She sent it and waited to see if there would be a reply. When none came, she placed her phone in the cup holder and finally backed out of her parking space.

"Janet? You're still here?"

Janet forced her attention away from the stapled papers in her hand and faced the front door of Debbie's Craftsman-style house. "I brought dinner."

The sensible shoes Debbie had worn to work that same day made soft clicking sounds as she advanced across the parlor's recently refurbished wooden floors.

"Really?" Debbie stepped into the kitchen with its new black-and-white linoleum.

Reluctantly, Janet set Joe Carter's paper on the vacant chair to her right and motioned toward the freshly set table. "I did. All you need to do is sit down."

"Why?"

"Because it's easier to eat sitting down," Janet quipped.

Debbie rolled her eyes. "No. Why did you bring me dinner, and"—she sniffed the air—"what on earth smells so good?"

"That would be my barbecue chicken."

"The recipe Tiffany loves so much?" Debbie asked.

"That's the one."

"Why aren't you eating it with her and Ian?" Debbie crossed to the closest of her new black granite countertops and lifted the slow cooker's lid. "That smells like heaven."

"Ian is covering for the media-relations officer at tonight's council meeting, and Tiffany is eating dinner with Ashling and her family."

"Yet you still made this?"

Janet stood, carried their empty plates to the counter, and filled them with tender chicken and the potato salad she'd gotten at the deli. "I didn't know about either conflict when I put it in the slow cooker this morning."

"Their loss is my gain." Debbie moved to the refrigerator and pulled it open. "What would you like to drink? Water? Milk? Soda?"

"Water works."

"Perfect." Debbie filled the glasses Janet had set out then joined her at the table, a quiet, yet unmistakable smile playing at the corners of her lips.

"I got your text about dropping off the cookies almost an hour and a half ago," Janet prodded.

A pinkish hue fanned outward across Debbie's cheeks. "Has it been that long?"

Janet looked down at her plate in an effort to shield her rapidly growing smile. "It has."

"I guess Greg and I chatted longer than I realized." Debbie folded her hands. She said a prayer of thanks for their meal and their friendship. When she was done, they both dug into the meal.

"This is so, so good, Janet. Thank you." Debbie stopped eating long enough to butter the corn bread Janet had also brought. "Did you get everything you wanted at the party store?"

"I did. And in the exact right shade of blue too." She decided to try again. "Did the boys like the cookies?"

Debbie set her fork down and leaned back in her chair with a satisfied smile. "They did. Very much."

"And Greg? Did he like them too?"

Debbie's smile spread to include her eyes. "He did. He said his mother used to make him chocolate chip cookies when he was growing up, and they reminded him of those."

"You must've talked about more than cookies if you were there for so long, right?"

"We did. He told me some more about his childhood, I told him some more about mine, and we sat on his front porch and enjoyed each other's presence."

"It sounds nice. Perfect, actually."

"It kind of was. Thanks for suggesting I take the cookies to them."

"My pleasure, my friend."

Debbie straightened. "Hey, I wanted to ask about that talk you were having with Audrey earlier, but I got sidetracked. Did you tell her what we think about her uncle being the family artist?"

"I did, but she insists that it wasn't him."

Debbie paused with a bite of chicken in midair. "That sounds pretty definitive."

"Because it is. His dominant side was injured in the war. His leg, his arm, his hand. He couldn't have copied a wartime film he wouldn't have seen until he got home, if he saw it at all. And the mouse pictures were dated 1944. He was already injured by then."

"That's upsetting," Debbie said, digging back into her meal. "How awful for him. And I thought we'd figured out the case of the unknown artist."

"I thought so too."

Debbie pointed at the papers next to Janet's spot. "Is that the paper Tiffany's professor gave you to read?"

"It is. And it's fascinating."

"Is it?"

Pushing the rest of her meal to the side, Janet reclaimed the stapled pages and flipped to the last page she'd read, about halfway through. "Joe's paper on the subject is so full of heart and so interestingly written that it's making me want to find out whether he teaches any online classes. I understand why Tiffany loved his class so much."

"For you to take in all your spare time, of course," Debbie teased before taking a bite of corn bread.

Janet chuckled. "I know. But listen to this part here. It's a quote he pulled from a newspaper article printed shortly after the start of the war." Janet took a drink of water and then began to read. "'Film, whether animated or not, speaks to the world in a different way than an article in a newspaper might. It shows rather than tells, and for young men thrust into war, seeing rather than hearing is easier to process.'"

"Makes sense," Debbie mused.

Janet skimmed the next paragraph and then said, "This is a quote from a woman named Cindy Galvin from the same article. 'That's what my son, Bobby, is doing. He's teaching the unthinkable in a way that's more palatable and will, in turn, hopefully bring more of our young soldiers home safely.'"

Debbie added a little more butter to her corn bread but stopped short of taking another bite. "This Bobby person was an animator, I take it."

"Joe doesn't have the whole article here, but based on what was said and the point of the paper, I think that's a fair assumption." Janet skimmed a few paragraphs ahead of where she'd been when Debbie arrived. "Yes, here we go. Another quote from Cindy Galvin mentions her son's work with Sunlight Studios."

Janet set down the paper and pulled out her phone. "I'm going to look that up."

She tapped away at her phone and studied her screen. "It was a film studio. In California."

"*Was?*" Debbie asked. "As in it doesn't exist anymore?"

"Correct."

"When did it close?"

Again, Janet looked at her screen and scrolled down. "In 1967. We need to keep that name in mind. I can't imagine there were many film studios in existence back then, let alone ones that made those short wartime animations."

"We're not going to research it right now." Debbie pointed her empty fork at Janet's plate. "Eat up before I help myself to your corn bread."

CHAPTER TWENTY-TWO

It was after nine when Janet slipped her key into the lock and stepped through her front door, her freshly washed slow cooker tucked under her left arm. Spying a pair of sneakers inside the entryway, she cocked her ear toward the bedroom hallway.

"Tiffany?" she called. "I'm home."

The words kicked off several sounds—the creak of a bed, the shuffle of slippers, and finally, the enthusiastic "Mom!" that always made Janet feel like she was on top of the world.

"Did you and Dad go somewhere?" Tiffany planted a kiss on Janet's cheek and then peered out the front window. "And why did you take both cars?"

Janet set her key ring on the catchall table beneath the light switch and headed toward the kitchen, Tiffany close on her heels. "The department's media-relations officer felt ill this evening, so your dad had to cover the monthly meeting at town hall. He should be back any minute now though."

"And you?" Tiffany asked.

"Since I had to stash all the paper products I bought for your dad's party at Debbie's, I decided to take dinner with me to her place." Janet opened the set of lower cabinet doors to the right of the oven. "I'm glad I did, because it's always nice spending time with her outside the café."

Tiffany reached out and stopped any further movement on Janet's part. "Whoa. You can't put the slow cooker away."

She looked back at her daughter. "Why not? It's clean."

"*Clean?*" Tiffany echoed in horror. "But I thought you were going to save some chicken for me."

Reaching past Tiffany, Janet set the pot on its proper shelf, wrapped the cord around its base, and stood, hands on hips. "And I did. A plate for you, and a plate for your dad—both wrapped and in the fridge."

"Oh. Good." Tiffany crossed to the refrigerator, peeked inside, and found proof of Janet's words. "Phew. You had me worried there for a second."

"As if I would ever let my family go hungry." Janet chuckled, then appraised her daughter. "So? Did you enjoy your dinner at Ashling's? Did you get to pick her uncle's brain about his career like you'd hoped?"

"It was great, Mom. I asked her uncle a ton of questions, and he was super cool about answering them. He even said I asked good ones."

"I'm sure you did," Janet said. "You're a smart girl, Tiffany Arabella Shaw."

Tiffany ducked her head. "Thanks, Mom."

"Thank *you*," Janet replied. "By the way, where are Ranger and Laddie? They didn't come to the door when I got home."

"They're cuddled up on my bed under the covers."

Janet nodded. "Reading in bed is their favorite time of day, no doubt."

"Actually, I wasn't reading. Not a book, anyway." Tiffany bounced on the balls of her feet. "I was hunting for some more present ideas for Dad, and I think I found something pretty perfect."

Janet felt hope rise once again. "Okay, don't keep me in suspense."

"You can get him a he shed!"

Janet stared at her. "A *he* shed? Aren't those usually for women?"

"They don't have to be. The point is that they're a personal space for someone who might enjoy that. He could watch TV, hang out with his friends, even put a dartboard or foosball table in there." Tiffany smiled triumphantly. "Whatever he wants, really, because it would be completely his space."

Janet leaned against the nearest countertop. "Tiffany, you are a genius. Truly."

"So you like the idea?"

"Like it? I think it's fantastic." Pushing away from the counter, Janet wandered over to the sliding glass door that led to the back deck. She bathed the backyard in light with the flip of a switch. There wasn't a lot of room. But a shed might fit where Tiffany's old playhouse had once been.

"You could hire Mr. Connor to build it, or at least ask him where you can get a ready-made one."

Janet imagined a small shed, painted to match the house, with a cute square window next to an attractive door, and masculine, perhaps Scottish, touches inside to make it truly Ian's. It would be a true escape for him.

If only they'd thought of it sooner.

"There's no way something like that could be ready in time for his birthday," Janet said glumly, switching off the deck light.

"True. But you could make a certificate telling him about it and put it in a card. Wait!" Tiffany grabbed Janet's arm. "You could put something about it on a tiny slip of paper and put it inside one of his favorite desserts. That way he *thinks* he's getting just that, but he's not."

"Tiffany, you're brilliant. This is finally something I think he'll really enjoy."

At the sound of Ian's key in the door, Janet held her finger to her lips and mouthed *thank you* to her daughter before hurrying into the living room.

"You're home." Janet waited for her husband to drop his keys next to hers and then stepped into his waiting arms. "Long meeting, huh?"

"You can say that again," he said against her hair.

"Long meeting, huh?" Tiffany joked.

"My little comic." Ian released Janet and yawned. "I can't tell you how good it feels to be home."

"Probably almost as good as it feels to have you home," Janet said, earning a playful eye roll from their daughter as she made her way back to her bedroom.

When Tiffany disappeared around the corner, Janet planted a kiss squarely on Ian's lips and then motioned toward the couch. "Our usual game shows are over, obviously, but we could find something to watch if you'd like?"

"Actually, if you don't mind, I think I'm ready to turn in for the night," Ian said with another, even bigger yawn. "That meeting went on, and on, and on."

"And on?"

"You have no idea," he said. "Some people really like to hear themselves talk."

Scooping up the folder she'd left on the entryway table, Janet followed Ian into the bedroom. While he got into his pajamas, she brushed her teeth and washed her face. And while he did the same, she put on her pajamas and got settled under the covers with the last few pages of Joe's paper.

World War II changed the nation's outlook on many things, including animation—an art form previously seen as nothing more than whimsical fun. In the wake of the attack on Pearl Harbor, what had previously been a means of entertainment became a way to reach the masses. For the government, animation became a medium to deliver propaganda to the public, as well as a way to boost morale. And the military used it as a vehicle for training and education on various war-related topics.

Suddenly, animators at movie studios were asked to use their skills for the good of their country. Among those who answered the call was Kenneth Hartman, a young animator at the beginning of his career. In what he described in an interview many years later as "the blink of an eye," Hartman went from knocking on studio doors in the hopes of finding work to being so busy he barely slept.

The bulk of his work during the war effort was spent crafting animation for soldiers. With the help of his many hand-drawn characters, Hartman taught young servicemen how to dress, how to use their weapons, what to do if captured, and how to avoid death.

His career took another turn two years later, when his first wartime animation for the public debuted. Need It?

Grow It *was an instant success. For the government, it was a huge help in showing the public how they too could help in the war effort in the most basic of ways—growing food for themselves and their communities. It earned Hartman his first award and ignited what went on to be an unforgettable post-war career in an art form he loved. And for Sunlight Studios, it—*

Janet rocketed up off her pillow. "Sunlight Studios," she murmured. "That's the studio that Bobby Galvin worked for. And it's the studio that made *Need It? Grow It.*"

"Talking to yourself?" Ian asked, exiting the bathroom.

"A little, I guess."

She glanced back at the paper. *And for Sunlight Studios, it was the true start to what became a long and lucrative partnership with their soon-to-be top animator, Kenneth Hartman.*

Ian settled in beside Janet. "Is that something important?"

She skimmed the last paragraph then placed the report on her nightstand. "It might be."

"That doesn't sound terribly convincing."

"Because I'm not convinced." She set her alarm, made sure her phone was charging, turned off the light, arranged her covers, and fluffed her pillow. Then she said, "Something is bothering me, and I'm not sure what it is."

She waited for Ian to question her words, to start a dialogue that would get to the bottom of whatever she couldn't quite put her finger on, but all she heard was the sound of a faint snore.

CHAPTER TWENTY-THREE

Kneeling on the grass, Janet noted the length as indicated by the tape measure and carefully wrote it on a loose sheet she'd grabbed from a notepad on her way out the door. Then, with a glance up at the house, she stood, moved the measuring device to cover the available width and—

"What are you doing out here?"

She snapped her gaze to the deck and felt her stomach clench. "Ian. Hi."

"I was getting some orange juice for the road when I saw something move out here. I thought Ranger had gotten out, but it's you. In the backyard with paper and a measuring tape."

Janet cast about for something, anything, she could say that wouldn't spoil the surprise of the gift. The only options that filtered through her thoughts, though, would be untruthful, and she refused to lie to her husband.

Finally, she threw up her hands. "Could you ask me something else, please?"

His left eyebrow arched, but he complied, tapping his watch. "What are you doing home at this time of the day? Shouldn't you be at the café?"

"Right. Yes. I should." Janet stuffed the tape measure into the front right pocket of her cargo pants, the paper and pencil into the left, and trotted toward the deck stairs. "Debbie and Paulette are covering for me. Time got away from me, I guess."

"It has a way of doing that, doesn't it?" Ian chuckled, then surveyed the yard. "Now that summer is right around the corner, I hope we'll get to spend more time out here. It's such a nice space."

She tried to hold back her answering smile, but when her effort proved futile, she turned her head as if to follow his gaze, hoping the movement would prevent him from spotting the smile. "Oh, you will."

"I said *we*, my love, not *me*."

"Right. Yes. *We*." She felt the weight of his gaze and willed herself to remain calm, to give nothing away.

Ian walked over to the deck railing and leaned against it. "I'm not saying I don't miss summers with Tiffany when she was little, but there's something special about being able to stand out here and enjoy our lawn without an inflatable pool and her old playhouse cluttering it up."

She swallowed. "That inflatable pool and playhouse gave you less grass to cut each week."

"True. But I don't mind cutting the grass—you know that," Ian said. "In fact, I'm pretty sure I've mentioned a time or two how therapeutic it can be."

"You have," Janet said, joining him at the railing. "But less grass to mow means more time sitting here on the deck, or watching sports on TV with your friends, or throwing some darts, or—"

"Throwing darts?" he echoed.

"You do that at work, sometimes, right? In the reserve room?"

"Once in a blue moon."

Janet faced him and fixed the collar of his shirt. "If you had less grass to mow, stuff like that wouldn't have to be confined to once in a blue moon. That's all I'm saying, Ian."

He flicked his hand toward the lawn. "Regardless, I'm glad we have an empty yard now, with nothing in the way. Means we have a lot less clutter in our line of sight when we're sitting out here on the deck, enjoying our property."

"Right," Janet managed to squeak past her rapidly dying hopes. "A lot less clutter."

Janet was a solid mile from the café when it finally dawned on her that she'd turned the wrong way at the end of her workday. The other direction would have taken her home or to the grocery store or even the ice cream parlor on an unusually hot day for May.

But while she might not have been conscious of that decision in the moment she'd made it, it had become quite intentional by the time she rounded the corner onto Morningside Court.

She still wasn't sure why she was showing up at Audrey Barker's house unannounced. Yet, there she was, parking in front of the woman's home anyway.

Janet shut off the engine and dropped the keys into her tote bag as she climbed out of the car. She had spent most of the day trying to lose herself in the café's busyness. But no matter how busy she'd made herself, her mind had wandered off, time and time again.

Some of that wandering had been to Ian, his rapidly approaching surprise party, and the doors that kept closing on every creative gift idea Tiffany put on her radar. But the vast majority of her wandering thoughts were on why she was there, making her way up Audrey's sidewalk instead of her own.

She knocked and then stepped back at the sound of approaching footsteps on the other side of the door.

"Janet!" Audrey exclaimed, pulling open the door to reveal an expression that moved from surprise to confusion and landed on...*worry*? "Goodness, did we plan to go through the rest of Mama's things this afternoon and I forgot?"

Raising her hands, Janet reassured her. "Not at all. This is definitely an impromptu visit. I was thinking about you a lot today and wanted to come talk to you. But I realize I should've called. I can come back later if this is a bad time."

Audrey stopped Janet's retreat with a beckoning finger. "Actually, I'm glad you're here. I have something to show you."

"Are you sure?" Janet asked. "I could see whatever it is at a different time—a time of your choosing."

"No, now is perfect. Come in, come in." Audrey stepped aside to allow Janet into her home. "I'm due to go to the grocery store tomorrow, but I have popcorn we could enjoy together."

Sheepishly, Janet trailed the woman down the hallway, shaking her head as she did. "Please. No fuss. It's bad enough I showed up unannounced." She smacked herself in the forehead. "I didn't even bring you treats from the bakery."

"Like I have so many other things to do. And I don't need more treats. You're already spoiling me rotten," Audrey said. "Honestly, you stopping by like this makes me feel as if I might have my first real friend here in Dennison."

"There's no 'might' about that."

"Thank you, dear." Audrey motioned toward the kitchen. "So? Popcorn? Soda? Water?"

"I'm okay, but thank you."

Audrey shrugged and led the way into the sun-soaked family room. Ushering Janet to the couch, she crossed to a card table covered with picture frames.

Carefully, Audrey picked up a frame and carried it over to the couch. "What do you think?" she asked, handing it to Janet.

Janet drew in a gasp at the beauty and quiet power of the final scene in Kenneth Hartman's *Need It? Grow It*. "I love this one."

"I do too." Audrey slowly lowered herself onto the cushion beside Janet and tilted her head for a better view of the drawing. "I love all the pictures, but this one makes me think of Mama. I can imagine her sharing her family's crops with little ones in the neighborhood. It's just the way she was."

Janet took in the rainbow stretching across the perfectly blue sky as the sun chased away a few stray clouds. Rows of plump strawberries filled the foreground, with blueberries ripening in the background. A parade of overflowing baskets and pails stood between them.

But the young woman still stole the scene, her expression lovely with kindness and generosity as she held one of the strawberries out to the little boy peering at her through the fence. The child's face was full of hope and joy.

"I can't imagine a person drawing something this amazing to begin with, let alone doing so after having only seen the original on a screen for no more than a few seconds," Janet murmured. "Even if she saw it multiple times."

Audrey flopped back against the couch. "It's really that close to the film you say it was based on?"

"It's spot-on," Janet said. "Uncannily so."

"Mama's parents were poor going into the war and even more so during the war," Audrey said. "So it's hard to imagine Mama seeing a movie in the theater. But how neat that someone—who'd clearly seen it often—drew it for her."

Janet reserved judgment on that. "You'll be able to see how accurate it is yourself in a few weeks."

"Really? How?" Audrey asked.

"Tiffany's professor from Case Western Reserve is lending his collection of wartime animated films to the museum here in Dennison for the summer. I'm sure *Need It? Grow It* will be among them." She handed the framed piece back to Audrey.

Audrey stared at it, her lips drawn tight in a pained line. "I just don't understand why she never showed us these. It would have been a fun thing to see from that time in history."

"I would imagine that after the death of three brothers and Everett's injuries, it became a very difficult time for her to remember, much less share with you," Janet said.

Audrey's expression softened as she met Janet's gaze. "I haven't thought of it from that perspective. But you're probably right."

"She endured a lot of pain for someone so young."

"She did," Audrey agreed quietly. She shook herself as if to remove the heaviness from their conversation. "If you're free for a little while longer, we could go up to the community firepit. I think I really would like to burn that rejection letter from Sunlight Studios. Mama didn't deserve that kind of cruelty."

"What?" Janet scooted forward so fast that her knee bumped Audrey's. "Sorry. But did you say Sunlight Studios?"

"Yes. That was the name of the studio that sponsored the contest Mama entered."

Janet gasped. "How do you know it was Sunlight Studios? I don't remember seeing that in the letter."

"I've spent more time with it than you have," Audrey said. "The letterhead is faded, but it's there, across the bottom."

Janet's thoughts raced in a million different directions before settling on one. "May I see the letter again?" she asked. She didn't know what she thought that would accomplish, but surely it couldn't hurt.

Audrey rose and set the frame back on the card table. "Of course you can see it, Janet. You helped me go through my mother's things so I wouldn't have to do it alone."

"That was my pleasure."

"A pleasure that took time away from your family." Audrey motioned for Janet to follow. "This way. It's still in the spare room."

Janet trailed Audrey down the hallway and into the spare bedroom. Like the first time she'd seen it, the same long card table stood beneath the room's lone window. But now, instead of the drawings that preceded the newly framed one, it held two things—a closed sketch pad and a box of pencils.

"Did you figure out what you want to draw?" Janet asked.

"No. I went through a few boxes I had in the closet though."

"That makes sense for now," Janet said. "But eventually you won't have any boxes left to unpack."

"Eventually." Audrey stepped over to the table, lifted the sketch pad, and retrieved the self-addressed stamped envelope they'd run across right before they found the letter. She handed it to Janet. "I think the letter must have come in this envelope, so that's where I've been keeping it."

Janet read Mae's name in both the center and upper left corner of the envelope then opened the flap to retrieve the rejection letter. Sure enough, printed across the bottom of the letter, in very faint letters, was the name *Sunlight Studios.*

She noted the address typed below it then turned her attention back to the response that had cut Audrey's mother to the core. The words that had stunned Janet on Monday now stirred a fierce anger inside her.

"I didn't even know your mother, and this letter enrages me," Janet said as she reached the end. "And for the person who wrote it to hide their cruelty behind an anonymous name like *Mystery Judge*? It's so wrong."

Audrey nodded. "It really is."

"We absolutely should burn this," Janet said, sliding it back inside the envelope. "There's no reason to keep something so terrible."

Audrey pursed her lips then said, "Then again, if Mama kept it, maybe I should too."

"That's up to you. But if you opt to keep it, I don't think you should keep reading it when it causes you pain. Unless it's motivating you to take your own drawing more seriously."

"I'm seventy-one."

"That shouldn't stop you." Janet lowered the envelope to the table and allowed her fingers to linger over the stamps in the upper-right corner. "Four stamps," she murmured.

Audrey's laugh held no sign of humor. "That's all it took for someone to destroy Mama's hopes and dreams."

Janet took one last look at the stamps and Mae's youthful handwriting on the envelope then set it down when her phone vibrated in her pocket. She glanced at the screen and excused herself to Audrey to answer the call. "Stacy, hello! How are you?"

"Busy in a good way. Getting everything ready for the exhibit is making me feel my grandfather's presence more than ever."

"How lovely."

"It is," Stacy said. "Anyway, I'm calling because I came across a necklace on the floor this afternoon that I don't recognize. I've been too busy for many guests recently, so I was wondering if it could be yours. It's a silver heart-shaped pendant on a thin silver chain, and it seems to have a faulty clasp."

Janet gasped. "I think it is."

"Here, let me take a picture, and I'll send it to you."

When the photo arrived, Janet confirmed it. "Yes, that's mine. It was a Mother's Day gift from my daughter several years ago. The clasp broke at work, and I put it in my purse until I could have it repaired. It must have fallen out of my purse when I gave you my business card. I've been so busy I didn't even realize it was missing."

"Then I'm glad to have found it before you discovered it missing and were worried. Especially since you wouldn't have been able to find it because it's been here all along. Should I mail it to the café address from your business card, or would you rather give me your home address and have me send it there?"

Janet opened her mouth to give her home address, but a glance at Audrey gave her a better idea. "Actually, would you have time for me to stop by again and pick it up? I'd love to bring my daughter, Tiffany, this time, as well as another friend. The two of them were instrumental in putting me onto your grandfather's work in the first place."

"I'd love that," Stacy answered.

"Fantastic. What works for you?"

"I'm free tomorrow after five."

She thought about the party prep that had to be done in the next week, calculated how she could fit it in around a drive to the Pittsburgh area, and—silently kicking herself—agreed to the meeting and ended the call.

"What was that about?" Audrey asked.

"I'm throwing a surprise party for my husband in a little over a week, I still have absolutely no idea what to get him as a present, and I just made plans to drive to Pittsburgh, ideally with you and Tiffany, after work tomorrow," Janet replied, rubbing the back of her neck. "I sound crazy even to myself."

"With me?"

"If you're free," Janet said. "That's where Stacy Hartman lives. She's the granddaughter of Kenneth Hartman, the animator responsible for *Need It? Grow It.*"

"I'm touched that you'd want me to come along, dear. I really am, but I signed up to try out a ladies' card night in the community center tomorrow evening."

"Oh, Audrey, I'm so glad to hear that. Truly."

Audrey ducked her head. "I almost didn't call about it, but then I did."

"Good for you."

"Time will tell." Audrey led Janet out of the room. "So, still no present, huh?"

"Nope. And I thought I had a really good one this morning before I left for work. But my husband let me know he's glad we're not shed people."

"Shed people?" Audrey echoed.

"He caught me measuring a spot for a he shed before I left for work. I didn't tell him what I was doing, but as always seems to be the case with Ian, it was like he knew, though I can never guess how."

A flash of amusement tugged at Audrey's lips as she led the way across the living room and over to the front door. "I guess that's good though, right? Saves you spending money on something he won't use."

"I guess. I want to give him something he'll love from the moment he sees it. But I don't want to bake it. And as sweet as it is every time he says it, *I* am not a birthday gift. Nor is our marriage. Neither can be wrapped, and he already has both of those. And we are years away from spending our fiftieth wedding anniversary in Scotland."

Audrey pulled the front door open. "For what it's worth, sometimes putting it out of your head for a little while can make all the difference. If you do, something might come to you during the drive tomorrow."

"And if it doesn't?" Janet asked. "What then? I need to have something for him."

"Then you put it in God's hands. He'll know what's best, as He always does."

CHAPTER TWENTY-FOUR

Janet smiled at her daughter in the passenger seat. Between her navigating skills and singing along with whatever song was on the radio, Tiffany had proven to be a wonderful driving companion. They'd talked about everything, from Tiffany's friends and classes at Case Western to the list of things she hoped to do with Ashling and her other friends before the end of summer. Janet had talked a little about her childhood and the café, and a lot about the party for Ian that would be happening in exactly one week.

"I'm glad you're able to come with me to Stacy's this time," Janet said as the current song ended.

Tiffany shut off the radio. "I am too. Especially after you told me about your first visit. I can't wait to see this stuff."

Janet moved into the right lane to take the next exit. "We're almost there."

"I'm sorry the clasp on the necklace I gave you broke like that, Mom."

Janet chuckled as they reached the traffic light at the end of the ramp. "Considering how much I've worn it since you gave it to me nine years ago, I'd say I'm lucky it lasted as long as it did." They pulled onto the same quiet road she remembered from the previous visit. "But it'll be an easy fix, I'm sure. I just need a moment to take it to the jeweler in New Philly that Debbie suggested. Something I will prioritize once your dad's party is behind me."

"I'm glad you love it so much, even after all this time." Tiffany peered out the window as Janet parked along the curb. "This is his granddaughter's house?"

Janet shut off the car. "It is. And I love that necklace so much because you picked it out by yourself, and when you gave it to me, you said you liked it 'because hearts mean love, and I will love you forever and ever.'"

"You remember what I said when I gave it to you?" Tiffany asked with a laugh as they climbed out of the car.

"Of course. How could I not with how cute it was?" She met Tiffany on the sidewalk, drew her close for a side hug, and kissed her temple. "I love you, sweetheart."

"I love you too, Mom."

Janet motioned toward Stacy's house. "You ready?"

"Absolutely."

When they reached the front door, Janet raised her hand to knock but dropped it back to her side as Stacy pulled it open.

"Janet, you made great time." Stacy aimed her welcoming smile at Tiffany. "Hi, I'm Stacy. You must be the famous Tiffany. Welcome."

Tiffany shook Stacy's outstretched hand then followed her into the house with Janet behind her. "I have to tell you, Stacy, that studying your grandfather was my favorite part of the film history class I took this past semester. It was so interesting to watch his growth throughout the war and then, later, everything he did afterward, both as himself and under his pseudonym."

"Thank you, Tiffany. That means a lot, especially from someone of your generation. It gives me hope that his legacy will live on." Stacy led the way to the room devoted to her grandfather's career and gestured to the framed pictures and the antique drawing table beyond. "Feel free to explore while I get your mom's necklace. I laid it on the kitchen table so it wouldn't get tangled."

Janet and Tiffany made their way into the room while Stacy retreated into the kitchen.

"Wow," Tiffany whispered. "This is so cool. Dr. Carter would love this."

Janet motioned her over to the award and the framed photo beside it. "I think you're right, which is why I'm hoping to connect him with Stacy. I know he'll enjoy the traveling exhibit this fall if he's able to go. But seeing all of this privately and having the chance to talk about it with the animator's own granddaughter would be really special for him."

"I'd like to attend the exhibit," Tiffany said.

"You can if you want to travel to it," Stacy said, joining them once more. "But, honestly, being here now will give you the chance to see even more than we'll display at the exhibit. I have to pare this down somehow to my grandfather's most important work. Janet, here's your necklace."

"Thank you so much." Janet took the necklace from Stacy, zipped it into a compartment inside her purse, and then pointed to the polished plaque in front of them. "Tiffany, this is the only award Kenneth Hartman got, and it's for the short you love so much."

"Actually, that was his only award for his *wartime* work," Stacy corrected kindly. "My grandfather actually went on to win many more over the course of his career."

Tiffany nodded. "I thought so. For his postwar stuff, right?"

"That's exactly right. You must have learned a lot about him," Stacy said, beaming.

"I had a good teacher who was very passionate about his work," Tiffany explained.

"I'm sorry. I didn't realize he'd won more awards." Janet directed her attention toward the framed photograph taken at the award ceremony. "Tiffany's response to *Need It? Grow It* was obviously shared by many at that time."

"You saw it." Tiffany glanced at Janet. "It was so powerful."

Stacy straightened the award picture then faced Tiffany. "Your mother told me your professor has a film collection from that time period, which has allowed both of you to watch my father's work the way people would have watched it at the time."

"That's true," Tiffany enthused. "And it was super cool. All of your grandfather's work was interesting, but *this* one"—she indicated the photo and the award—"had such a different feel."

"It was the one that led to his many postwar awards," Stacy said.

Janet gazed from the photo of the animator with his solemn expression to the actual award he'd been holding on that day.

Kenneth Robert Hartman
Animator, Sunlight Studios
Award of Merit for Outstanding Achievement
1946

"Was he a shy man?" Janet asked, glancing back at the photo.

Stacy tilted her head as if weighing Janet's question. "I don't think I'd call him *shy*. Though I can see why you might think that from this picture. Since he was still relatively new in his career at the time, he was probably uncomfortable with people making a fuss over him. Especially about something to do with the war."

It made sense.

So did the way Tiffany, who'd spotted Kenneth Hartman's writing desk, was moving toward it as if in a trance.

"Was this the actual workspace where he drew all his stuff?" Tiffany asked as she stopped mere inches from it. When Stacy confirmed it, Tiffany leaned over the desk. "Dr. Carter, my professor, would really, really love this. Can I take a picture of it to send to him?"

At Stacy's easy agreement, Tiffany took out her phone and snapped a picture of the desk. "Wow. So cool."

"Would you like to see more?" Stacy asked.

Tiffany's face lit up. "Yes, please."

As she'd done for Janet and Debbie on their previous visit, Stacy opened the drawers in the desk, retrieved the same stacks of sketch pads and cel folders she'd shown Janet, and carried them to the kitchen table, where for the next forty minutes she took Tiffany through the beginning of her grandfather's career.

"I knew it when I first saw them, but, wow, those pictures we found in Audrey's mother's things really are perfect copies, aren't they, Mom?"

"Pictures?" Stacy asked.

Janet nodded. "I told you about them the first time I visited. Tiffany and I found them when we were helping a friend sort through her late mother's possessions. Those drawings first alerted me to your grandfather and his work."

"I thought they were simply based on *Need It? Grow It*," Stacy said.

"They were," Janet said. "Only they're perfect copies of your grandfather's work, as Tiffany said."

"And your friend's mother drew them?"

"We're actually not sure who the artist was. But whoever *did* draw them clearly watched the film many, many times, because they're identical to the colorized version in your grandfather's cels. But they're sketches."

The color drained from Stacy's cheeks. "Sketches?" she echoed. "Of *Need It? Grow It*?"

"*Colored* sketches," Janet corrected.

Stacy blew out a breath. "Oh. Okay. I thought—" She waved her hand. "It doesn't matter."

"Trust me, I thought the same thing on the way home from my last visit. Lost some sleep over the possibility, in fact. But then Tiffany explained the various stages of animation and that color came into play at the cel stage of your grandfather's process."

Tiffany tapped the open sketch pad in front of her then the accompanying cels beside it. "That's how it was done for this, as you can see. My professor specialized in your grandfather's work, so he covered that process in class and specified that Mr. Hartman never added color before the cel stage."

Stacy's posture softened. "Right. I knew that. I'm sorry for jumping to conclusions."

"No worries," Janet said. "Like I said, it went through my head as well. Your family was wronged, after all. It's understandable that you'd want answers for that and be eager to find them."

"I still can't believe someone would steal his sketch pad for *Need It? Grow It*," Tiffany said as Stacy gathered both piles for their return to her grandfather's desk. "Who would do that?"

"My guess is someone who was jealous of the attention my grandfather received for that film," Stacy said. "Because, really, it was that change in direction that ultimately led to him being Sunlight Studio's top animator during their remaining years."

Janet scooped up the pile of sketch pads and carried them back to the drawing table while Tiffany trailed her with the cels.

When the items were safely in their assigned drawers, Stacy asked Tiffany, "Any interest in seeing some of Grandpa Ken's later sketch pads?"

"As Bobby Galvin?" Tiffany asked. "Absolutely! That would be—"

"*Bobby Galvin*?" Janet repeated.

Stacy met Janet's confusion with a knowing smile. "My grandfather started his career with his given name, Kenneth Hartman. But after the success of *Need It? Grow It*, he decided he should use a different name for his lighter stuff moving forward. The name he chose was a nod to his mother, my great-grandmother, who always believed in him."

"Correct me if I'm wrong, Stacy, but Bobby was the nickname she'd called him his whole life, and Galvin was her maiden name, right?" Tiffany interjected.

"Exactly. She went back to Galvin after she and my great-grandfather went their separate ways when my grandfather was in high school." Stacy smiled at her. "Your professor was clearly very thorough in his teaching."

"He had a soft spot for your grandfather's work, and he passed it on to me."

"Okay, I understand why he used Galvin. But where did the name Bobby come from?" Janet asked.

Across the hallway from the kitchen, Stacy opened a brown filing cabinet to reveal more sketch pads. "It came from his middle name, Robert. His father was Kenneth as well, so I guess they used Bobby around the house as a way to avoid confusion." She scooped several sketch pads into her arms then led them back to the kitchen table. "These are from his postwar work."

"Bobby Galvin," Janet murmured. "That name sounds so familiar to me."

"I probably mentioned it to you, Mom."

"Earlier this evening, you said he used a pseudonym for his later stuff, but you didn't say what it was, and—ah!" Janet snapped her fingers. "I remember. In an article Joe Carter referenced in his college paper, a woman named Cindy Galvin was quoted about her son—an animator she called Bobby. She must have been your great-grandmother, Stacy."

Stacy plucked the top sketch pad from the new pile and opened it between Tiffany and Janet. "I think I know the article you're talking about. Great-Grandma Cindy was very proud of my grandfather's work during the war."

"And rightfully so," Janet said, gazing at the initials *BG* worked into a crop of grass.

Stacy set the rest of the sketch pads within arm's reach of Janet and crossed to the same filing cabinet. "Grandpa Ken not only did his best to keep soldiers safe through his earliest animation, he also found a way to empower those back on the home front through the gentle, calming genius that was *Need It? Grow It*. But that's not all he did." She opened another drawer, rummaged around inside it, and returned with two sheets of paper. "He also did what he could to find others who could help wartime efforts through animation."

Tiffany turned to the next sketch in the pad. "That's right. He taught animation workshops, didn't he?"

Stacy held up one of the pieces of paper—a flyer announcing a month-long round of animation classes set to start on October 10, 1942. The instructor was Kenneth Hartman, a junior animator with Sunlight Studios.

"Wow." Tiffany admired the flyer. "This is the actual one from back then?"

Stacy nodded. "Grandpa Ken also served as a first-round judge for a contest the studio did to find new talent the following January. See?"

As she read the contest announcement, Janet sucked in a breath.

Good at drawing? Eager to do your part for the war effort?
Sunlight Studios wants to see what you can do!
Submit your best wartime work to:
R. Galvin, first-round judge

C/O Sunlight Studios
1451 Wright St.
Los Angeles, CA

"R. Galvin?" Janet asked, willing her voice to remain steady.

"Although he wasn't using the name Bobby Galvin yet for his work in 1943, I imagine he didn't want to link his name to the judging," Stacy said. "And I'm guessing he went with his initial to be more formal."

"He was a first-round judge," Janet said, staring at the contest announcement.

"He'd only been there a year," Stacy said.

Janet licked her lips in an attempt to fight the dryness spreading through her mouth and throat.

The top 5 entries will move on to a second-round judge. One lucky winner will be given the opportunity to meet with a Sunlight Studios animator to learn more about the craft and to discuss possible inclusion of the winning entry in the war effort!

**Deadline for entries is Jan. 29, 1943.

***Be sure to include a self-addressed, stamped envelope for the return of your materials.

Good luck and Godspeed,
The Sunlight Studios team

"This is so cool," Tiffany said. "Cool that you still have it, and cool that he did what he could to help someone else realize the same dream he'd had."

Pressing her hand against her stomach, which roiled with nerves, Janet pushed back her chair and stood. "Stacy, I'm sorry, but I—I just realized how late it's getting, and we've got a very long drive ahead of us."

"Mom?" Rocketing up from her own chair, Tiffany grabbed hold of Janet's arm. "Are you okay? You're pale all of a sudden."

"I'm fine, Tiffany. Really." Janet swallowed, forcing herself to breathe in and out, in and out. "But we should help put these sketch pads back where they go and then be on our way. We've taken enough of Stacy's time this evening, and I do have to get up early for the café."

Tiffany glanced out the window. "Mom's right. It *is* getting dark, and she goes into work at a time no human being should be awake. Except my dad, who also goes to work at the crack of dawn."

Understanding crossed Stacy's face. "I get it. And I'll take care of putting everything back where it belongs."

"Are you sure?" Tiffany asked, closing the sketch pad with obvious regret. "Because I don't mind helping."

Taking a chance while Stacy was engrossed in collecting the sketch pads, Janet brought her lips to her daughter's ear. "We need to leave," she whispered. "*Now.*"

CHAPTER TWENTY-FIVE

ait." Tiffany frowned at the image of Mae's rejection letter on her mother's phone. "I don't get why you think Stacy's grandfather wrote this letter to Audrey's mom."

Janet merged onto the highway toward Dennison and switched over to cruise control, lest her emotions affect the gas pedal. "Because he was the first-round judge in the contest she entered."

"How do you know it was the same contest? Sunlight Studios probably held lots of them."

With her eyes still on the road, Janet quickly pointed her daughter's attention back to the picture on her screen. "Read the date."

"February 15, 1943," Tiffany said, her voice faltering.

"The deadline on the contest flyer Stacy showed us was late January that same year. Therefore, it stands to reason the rejection letter is from that contest."

"Okay. But maybe—" Tiffany stopped then shook her head. "No, forget that. That wouldn't make sense."

Janet looked across the seat at her daughter. "What wouldn't make sense?"

"I was going to say the second-round judge could have written this, but clearly Mae's entry didn't make it that far." Slouching in her seat, Tiffany stared down at the image again. "But how could someone who crafted such a heartwarming film like *Need It? Grow It* write something as cruel as this? To someone who was maybe just like him?"

It didn't make sense.

"I wish Audrey's mother had saved her entry instead of this mean letter," Tiffany said.

"I wish so too, but I imagine that after reading that response to it, she probably threw it away."

Tiffany stuck Janet's phone into the empty cup holder between them and pulled her foot up onto the passenger seat. "I did that once. With a picture I made in second grade that a boy in my class made fun of."

"I didn't know that."

"I know. I didn't tell you."

"Why not?" Janet asked.

Tiffany turned toward her. "I guess I didn't want you to think it was bad too."

"Do you ever remember a time I didn't like something you drew or wrote or did in any way at home or school?"

"No. But I was eight, Mom." She laughed. "Don't worry. I've managed to get over it."

They drove in silence for a while before Janet remembered something from the previous afternoon. "Audrey framed the sketch of the last image from *Need It? Grow It*. She said that since it clearly meant something to Mae, she wants to hang it in the bedroom that would have been Mae's if she were still alive. But after what we just discovered about the man responsible for the short those sketches were based on, I'm mighty tempted to call her and tell her to take it down."

"Yeah, I can see that. I love his work, but after reading the letter he wrote, it doesn't feel the same."

After another mile or two of silence, Janet nudged her chin in the direction of the radio. "Want to listen to some tunes for a while? I think singing along to things will help keep me awake."

"You'll get no argument from me where music is involved." Tiffany turned on the radio and switched stations until she found one playing "Somewhere Over the Rainbow," which they both loved.

They sang along to the beloved classic, but it was a little sadder than usual, especially when Janet recalled the rainbow in the framed sketch at Audrey's house.

When the song ended, Tiffany switched off the radio. "Was Audrey able to flatten out the crease enough before she framed it?"

"Crease?" Janet asked, stifling a yawn.

"On the drawing of that last scene from *Need It? Grow It.*"

Janet pictured the framed drawing Audrey had proudly shown her the previous day. "I don't remember a crease, so she might have stacked some heavy books on top of it for a while or something before she put it in the frame. I think the line would still be visible though."

Tiffany took a pack of gum from the center console and popped a piece into her mouth. "The same crease ran down the center of every one of those drawings we found. As if they'd been folded together like you'd do if you wanted to stuff them into something."

"Oh, right. I remember what you're—" The rest of Janet's answer fell away in favor of a strangled gasp.

"Mom?" Tiffany asked. "What's wrong?"

"The drawings, Tiffany. They'd been *folded together.*"

Tiffany laughed. "I feel like I just said that."

"Like you'd do if you wanted to stuff them into something," Janet said.

"Are we playing the parrot game?" Tiffany asked, frowning.

Janet shook her head. "No, it's what you said."

"Which is the object of the parrot game—a game I could outlast you and Dad on every time we played it. I'm the undefeated champion," Tiffany said.

"No. We're not playing," Janet hastily said. "It's what you said about those drawings you found having been folded together. What if they were like that from being stuffed inside an envelope?"

Tiffany shrugged. "Sure, that could make sense. Probably to keep them together during a move or something."

"Audrey and I found a big manila envelope in the same box as that rejection letter from Sunlight Studios," Janet went on. "A *self-addressed, stamped* envelope like the contest required."

"Okay?"

Janet pulled up to the final stop sign on their route. "It was postmarked from California, and there were four three-cent stamps on it."

"That doesn't sound like much. I'm always amazed by how inexpensive things were back then, even adjusting for inflation."

"I'd have to do some checking, but one of those stamps was probably enough for two or three pieces of paper in 1943," Janet said. "Yet there were four of them."

"The contest said the entry would be returned if it didn't win, didn't it?" Tiffany asked.

"It did. And we know from that awful letter that Mae didn't win. Yet there were no drawings with the letter."

"Honestly, I still think she probably threw her entry away. Like I did with my picture when I was eight."

Janet heard her daughter's words, even registered them on some level, but—

"That's it!" she cried.

Tiffany jumped in her seat. "What?"

"What if those sketches we thought were copies of *Need It? Grow It* weren't actually copies? What if they were the original form of that short film?"

"We've been over this, Mom. And you saw it yourself at Stacy's. Color for Kenneth Hartman's work wasn't added until the cel stage. The whole studio probably did it that way too."

"Did you know that was the process before you took that class with Dr. Carter?" Janet asked as she pulled into their driveway.

"No. But anyone in that field would probably know."

"If they were already in that field, sure. But if they weren't? If they were simply putting their best foot forward for a contest?"

Tiffany stared at Janet. "Whoa. Are you saying what I think you're saying?"

Was she?

Was it even possible? Especially with how adamant Audrey had been from the beginning that it wasn't?

She thought back to the sketches, the rejection letter, and the stamped envelope then closed her eyes against the shiver that followed. "I think I am."

CHAPTER TWENTY-SIX

*J*anet ended the call and stared up at the ceiling. She'd tried to sleep after getting home with Tiffany the night before, with limited success. She'd tried to push away the nagging thoughts that made her move through the bulk of her Saturday on autopilot. But it had been no use.

Now, after her call with Audrey, everything she suspected and feared—much as she tried to dismiss it, citing an overactive imagination—appeared not only possible but probable.

The question of what to do with those suspicions, though, was making it difficult to breathe. Was it possible to confirm the truth when none of the people involved were even alive? And if she could confirm the truth and her suspicion was correct, well, what would that accomplish? Such a revelation would prove—

"Janet?"

Lowering her chin, she slid her gaze toward the front door and the uniformed man who stood there, watching her with concern.

"Ian." She scooted forward on the couch but stopped short of actually standing, the fog in her brain making it difficult to fully process his presence. "I didn't hear you come in."

"So I noticed." Ian took off his hat, set it on the catchall table, and crossed to the couch. "You didn't even realize I was in the room until the fourth time I said your name."

She shook her head, trying to loosen the mental fog, but it didn't budge. "I'm sorry, Ian. It's not about you."

"Is it about yesterday's drive and how late you got home?"

Janet nodded.

"Did you and Tiffany have some sort of disagreement? Was there an issue with the car?"

"No," she said. "It's nothing like that."

He sank onto the cushion beside her. "Hey," he said, spotting the phone on her lap, "is this about a call?"

She felt him squeeze her hand, heard the worry in his voice. "The call certainly didn't help."

"It sounds like you should start at the beginning."

She collapsed back against the couch with a groan. "Remember those drawings Tiffany and I found in Audrey Barker's storage area a few weeks ago?"

"The ones in her mother's things that she knew nothing about? The ones you were afraid had been stolen from that animator, but it turns out they weren't because of something to do with color and when it was added?"

She nodded. "Yeah, those."

"What about them?"

"Remember that rejection letter Audrey's mother received from a drawing contest she'd entered as a teenager?"

Ian frowned. "Yes."

"It was a contest sponsored by Sunlight Studios, a place that closed down in the late sixties," Janet said. "The studio made many of the animated wartime short films that Tiffany's professor will have on display at our museum this summer."

"Okay."

"The animator's name was Kenneth Hartman. I visited his granddaughter with Debbie a while back, then again last night with Tiffany. He made the film that matched those drawings we found in Mae's things." She bit her lip. "He was the first-round judge for that contest Mae entered in 1943."

Ian gaped at her. "Wait. Does that mean this Kenneth guy is the one who wrote that nasty rejection letter?"

She nodded. "I believe he was."

Ian gave a long, low whistle. "Not cool."

"I think it gets worse," she told him. "Much, *much* worse."

"What could be worse?" he asked, his eyes wide.

"Tiffany and I saw the contest flyer from 1943. As part of the submission process, entrants needed to include a self-addressed, stamped envelope to either alert the winner about their success or to send back the entry along with a rejection letter, as was the case for Mae."

Ian crossed his arms and waited.

"Along with the rejection letter, Audrey and I found a large, empty envelope."

"Self-addressed and stamped, right?" Ian mused.

"Yes. It had multiple stamps—four to be exact." Janet absently traced her finger around her phone's case as she thought back on her recent call with Audrey—the information she'd learned sending a fresh shiver down her spine. "One stamp would have likely been enough for the rejection letter alone. Four of them would have been what she needed for her entry to be returned if it didn't win."

"A good guess, I'm sure."

"I'm pretty sure I'm right. Especially after Audrey weighed it."

"I didn't realize you'd found the entry that had been rejected so harshly. That's amazing, right?"

"We didn't realize we had either," Janet hedged. "If I'm even right, and I might not be."

"You've lost me, Janet."

"Those drawings Tiffany and I found that first day were folded together down the center. You know, as if they'd been packed together at some point."

"Okay."

"I called Audrey and asked her to fold them all together again, the way they had been. Including the one she'd framed."

"Okay," he said again.

"She weighed them on her kitchen scale. With the envelope. And with the rejection letter."

Ian's gaze snapped to hers. "Let me guess. It would have cost about four stamps back then?"

"We think so," Janet confirmed.

"Whoa." Ian stood and began to pace. "So that short film, the one you and Tiffany liked so much—you think Audrey's mother is actually the one who drew it?"

"I do. And I think Audrey is starting to suspect it too."

He continued to pace, the same possibility that had wrought havoc inside her heart for the last day or so claiming his expression. "So you think the sketches were stolen, but not in the way you'd originally thought?"

"Exactly." Janet felt Ranger's nose against her thigh and slid her hand onto his back for the pets she'd been neglecting. "The normal process for animated films at that studio was for the first round to be sketches in black-and-white. The next round had the sketch being traced onto the cel and *then* colored."

Ian paused beside the edge of the couch. "Yet the drawings you found were already colored."

"They were. And I think they were because Mae was a teenager," Janet said. "She probably didn't know how things were done, or maybe she wanted to put her best foot forward with her contest entry." She thought for a moment. "My guess is that Kenneth Hartman made up the story of the stolen sketches to cover up the fact that he didn't have them. He must have copied Mae's colored pictures right to cels and skipped that step."

"Makes sense."

Janet massaged her temples. "Yep. Unfortunately, I think so too."

"*Unfortunately*?" Ian echoed. "Why unfortunately? This might finally get rid of Audrey's reluctance to draw once and for all. Isn't that a good thing?"

She hadn't thought of that. But that *would* be a positive if her suspicions were, in fact, correct. Thus far, all she'd been able to see was the potential downside. And it was a doozy.

"If I'm right, such a revelation will not only alter history, but also a granddaughter's opinion of her much loved and respected grandfather," Janet said. "I don't want to be responsible for bringing that to light."

Slowly, Ian lowered himself next to Janet, his hand finding hers once again. "I hadn't considered that."

Janet blinked rapidly against the tears welling in her eyes. "Stacy is so proud of her grandfather, Ian. So eager to have his story and his contributions be seen and appreciated by people today. It's why she's so excited about the traveling exhibit set to open this fall. She wants people to see what her grandfather did during such a pivotal time in our nation's history." She swiped at a tear that made its way down her cheek despite her best efforts. "I'm going to hurt her if I'm right about this."

"Yes, she'll be hurt," Ian said. "But not by you. By *him*."

Janet sniffed and wiped her other cheek. "Stacy adores that man. And she should. He was her grandfather, and it sounds like he was a good one. How can I poison her love for him, even if it's with the truth?"

"But if Audrey's mother is the one who truly created the artwork and Stacy's grandfather is getting all the credit, continuing that lie by way of an exhibit isn't fair to Audrey or her mother's memory. The pain is already in the world. It's simply misplaced right now."

Ian was right.

She just hoped *she* was wrong.

"I need to go back to Stacy's," she murmured. "After church tomorrow."

Ian wiped another tear from Janet's face. "I understand. Do what you need to do." Ian rested his forehead against Janet's. "For what it's worth, if this plays out the way you're thinking it will, you'll be doing the right thing in revealing the truth."

"Then why do I feel so awful?" Janet whispered.

CHAPTER TWENTY-SEVEN

*J*anet felt dreadful, and with each and every footstep toward the maroon-colored door with its patriotic wreath, that dread was magnified tenfold. But there was no turning back.

Not now.

Not after driving so far.

Not after thinking through everything Ian had said.

And not after Pastor Nick's sermon that morning from the book of John.

"'Then you will know the truth, and the truth will set you free,'" she repeated aloud from memory.

If Kenneth Hartman had stolen Mae Barker's art to pass off as his own, that truth would affect more than the history of animation. More importantly, it would change things for two women in two very different ways.

For Audrey Barker, learning that her mother had not only shared her own dream of being an artist but had also been good enough at it to earn accolades near and far—though they had gone to someone else—had the power to inspire and encourage.

For Stacy Hartman, learning of her grandfather's deceit could permanently alter the memory of a relationship from which she took great comfort.

At the base of the steps that led to the door, Janet paused and lifted her gaze to the sky. "Please, God," she whispered, "help me to know what the truth is. And help me to do what's right."

Slowly she climbed the steps, crossed the front porch, and knocked on Stacy's door, trying to ignore the heavy pit of dread in her stomach. She heard footsteps within and did her best to square her shoulders. No matter what, the visit would be a difficult one.

The door swung open.

"Hello again, Janet." Stacy stepped back, waved Janet inside, and then closed the door behind them. "For your sake, I hate that you made that long drive again, but selfishly, I'm so grateful that you did. I'm starting to feel a bit overwhelmed about all of this."

She directed Janet's attention to a series of crates—both large and small—lined up along the hallway. "What are those for?" Janet asked.

"The organizers for my grandfather's exhibit sent them yesterday. I have two weeks to get them sent back with the things I want displayed, but I'd rather get it done sooner if I can." Stacy released a quiet squeal. "Mainly because I'm excited and just want it to happen—even though the start date won't change whether I do this in the requested two weeks or before bedtime tonight."

Even knowing what she suspected to be true, Janet found it hard not to smile at the young woman's enthusiasm. "Have you gotten to those journals your grandfather kept during his career?" she forced herself to ask.

Stacy led the way to the room that held the relics of her grandfather's storied career, laid out in an order Janet couldn't decipher, and rested her hand on top of the same stack of sketch pads Tiffany had viewed with such joy less than forty-eight hours earlier. "Not yet. I stayed up late last night making a list of all the things I need to get in the crates. With church this morning, all I've packed is Grandpa Ken's award, the framed article and picture from when he got it, and the coordinating cels."

Instinctively, Janet's gaze traveled to the two blank spots on the left wall. "You're packing by project?"

"I wasn't aware that's what I was doing, but yes, I guess I am." Stacy opened the top sketch pad on the stack, studied it for a split second, and then quickly located the cels that correlated with the project. "I think that should make it easier for the handlers on the other end. Don't you?"

"I'm sure," Janet agreed. Then she forced herself to add, "I would imagine you'll want to include the journals he kept while working on his various wartime projects, right?"

"I don't know, but I'm leaning that way. I'm worried they might get damaged somehow."

Janet tried to clear her throat of its lump with a cough. "I don't know if the exhibitors would put the actual journal out. If you express your concern, they would probably copy an excerpt and put it in a frame alongside the more official information about each project."

Stacy paused in her organizational efforts to consider Janet's words. "You're right. I'm worrying needlessly. It would be neat for people to see how he got to each project."

"I'm guessing, since you already packed up the award and newspaper article for *Need It? Grow It*, you did the same with its journal?" Janet asked.

Moving on to the next sketch pad in the stack, Stacy quickly paired it with its proper cels. "Grandpa Ken didn't do a journal for *Need It? Grow It.*"

Janet felt her heart rate accelerate. "He didn't? Why not?"

Stacy paired another sketch pad and another series of cels. "I imagine because of the war and being extra busy."

"So, he didn't journal *any* of his wartime projects?" Janet asked.

"He did one for his soldier-aimed projects. Probably because it helped him cope with such dark material." Stacy matched another sketch pad with its cels. "It—along with the rest of his journals—are fascinating, if you're interested."

"Interested?" Janet echoed. "You mean, in *reading* them?"

"I don't see why not. I trust you."

Trying to hide how the words twisted the dagger in her heart, Janet replied, "I'd love to. If you really don't mind."

Stacy abandoned her work with the stack, crossed to the brown filing cabinet, and reached into the bottom drawer. "Off the top of my head, I'm not sure which is the one for the soldier films, but you'll find it as you go. And when you do, please set it aside for me to include in one of the crates."

"Have you read every one of these?" Janet asked, taking the pile from Stacy.

"All but the last one." Stacy smiled. "It was locked, and I didn't find the key until I came across it while setting up this room. With everything going on, I haven't had time to give it the attention I want to."

Janet fanned the books out like a deck of cards. "Would you rather I wait to read that one until you have?"

"No, that's okay. Read whatever you want in any or all of them, but I do recommend that you read them in order. It's more interesting that way."

Stacy returned to the table and the sketch pads, and Janet took a seat in the desk chair.

Late morning morphed into early afternoon as Janet flipped through Kenneth Hartman's journals—a collection of doodles, expressions, and arrows pointing from drawn snippets he consolidated into one. There were descriptions of scenes and people that found their way into sketches on later pages. And sometimes the animator appeared to work his way through various ideas and concepts in a stream of consciousness, sharing his thoughts, his hopes, and his frustrations as he went.

The third book in was the one from the war. As Stacy had mentioned, the doodles and expressions contained on its pages were indeed dark. He sketched the various parts of weapons. He practiced facial expressions one might use while holding a gun, cleaning a gun, and putting on a uniform for the first time.

"I found the wartime one." Janet closed the book and held it up for Stacy to see. "And you're right. It must have brought him to some very dark places."

Stacy, who'd moved on to other aspects of her grandfather's work, grimaced at the journal. "I can't imagine what that must've been like."

Early afternoon became midafternoon as Janet worked her way through more of Kenneth Hartman's career. It was fascinating to see how the man had honed his talent as he went, how his characters' lines softened, how his plans at the beginning of a project played out by the end.

She set down the second-to-last journal and reached for the final one—the one with the lock, the one Stacy herself had yet to read.

It followed a similar pattern to the others. Thoughts and ideas, some vague doodling, more serious drawings, and finally a few paragraphs about the character and what made him or her tick.

She turned the page, her gaze falling on two paragraphs, written in the same handwriting as the other pages, but messier and more hurried. The entry was dated one week before his death.

Tilting the book to afford herself as much of the light coming through the window as possible, Janet began to read.

"Why was It's Good to be Sam *your last animated short?" I get that question often, even after all these years.*

Sam, with his big, hope-filled eyes, sleepy smile, inherent clumsiness, and desire to do good even when he didn't always succeed, was ready for retirement. As was I.

Looking back, I'm proud of Sam, but I'm not proud of myself.

I could've been. I should've been. But I'm not. Because Sam only came to be on the screen because of the young woman I stole my first award-winning piece from. The award I won truly belonged to her. The praise I received was meant for her. The opened doors that eventually enabled me to bring Sam to life on the screen—they were hers to walk through, not mine.

The why is simple, yet ugly.

I was a man, soon to be tasked as a provider. She was a young girl, a teenager. She'd grow up, get married, and have a family. She'd be fine. She didn't need to worry about a career. Her dream couldn't be as important to her as mine was to me.

How wrong I was. About all of it. Her life's path wasn't mine to decide. I see that now. No. I'm ashamed to admit, I saw it then. I just didn't care.

I hope the work I did in its wake—the smiles it inspired, the bad days my characters transformed into happy ones— made up for some of it. I hope the values I instilled in my son and the way I taught him to be a better person made up for some of it as well.

But I'll never atone for all of it. I'm so very sorry. To Mae, and to my family who thinks I'm someone I'm not.

Janet gasped. Her worst fears were here, confirmed in Kenneth Hartman's own writing. "So it's true," she whispered. "It really was Mae's work."

"Who's Mae?"

Startled by the voice that wasn't her own, Janet's gaze snapped from Kenneth's journal entry to Stacy's curious expression as she studied her from behind the long table. Janet closed her eyes, recalling Ian's words.

"If Audrey's mother is the one who truly created the artwork and Stacy's grandfather is getting all the credit, continuing that lie by way of an exhibit isn't fair to Audrey or her mother's memory."

"Janet?" Stacy pressed. "Who's Mae?"

Wrapping her arms around the journal, Janet stood and met Stacy at the table. "Do you remember me telling you about those sketches that were copies of *Need It? Grow It*? The ones that were identical to your grandfather's cels?"

"I do. You and Tiffany found them in a box of personal effects belonging to your friend's mother, right?"

"Yes, that's right. My friend's name is Audrey, and her late mother's name was Mae." Janet swallowed. "Anyway, Audrey's childhood dream was to be an artist, but Mae steered her in another direction."

"How sad." Stacy perched on the edge of a nearby chair. "I can't imagine directing someone away from their dream."

Janet took a deep breath. "We now know that Mae did that as a way to protect Audrey."

"From chasing a dream?" Stacy asked.

"From being hurt the way she had been."

Stacy frowned in confusion. "I don't understand."

"Mae too had dreams of being an artist. An animator, actually." Janet held the journal out to Stacy. "I think you need to read your grandfather's final entry in his last journal. For Mae, and for Audrey."

Stacy stared at Janet. "What do your friend and her mother have to do with my grandfather?"

"Read it," Janet repeated. "I think he wanted you to."

"But—"

Janet stood and laid a gentle hand on the younger woman's shoulder. "I'm going to leave you alone and head back to Dennison. Call me when you're ready to talk about the best way to handle all of this. And Stacy?"

"Yes?"

"I'm so sorry." With that, Janet left.

CHAPTER TWENTY-EIGHT

Ian's surprise party was a smashing success. Janet could see it in the smiles on every face in the café. She could hear it in the pockets of animated chatter and bursts of laughter that surrounded her on all sides. And she felt it in every amused shake of Ian's head whenever he managed to catch her eye in the wake of his entrance and the shouts of *Surprise!* and *Happy Birthday!* that had greeted him.

"It's official," Debbie said, joining Janet. "You knocked this surprise party out of the park. As I knew you would."

She pulled Debbie in for a hug. "Thanks, in no small part, to you."

"I didn't do much other than give you a place to hide the paper products and the decorations—which look spectacular, I might add."

"Thanks to you and your idea to do a Scotland theme." Janet stepped back and smiled at her best friend. "And you did way more than merely provide a place to hide things."

Debbie flashed a smile in Ian's direction then lowered her voice so only Janet could hear. "Did you figure out a present for him?"

Janet smiled. "I did." She pointed to the table that was crammed with Ian's favorite muffins, pies, cakes, and pastries. "I finally decided to listen to my husband and believe what he was telling me."

Debbie gave her another hug and then dodged around pockets of guests toward the party's newest arrival. Janet watched Greg return her best friend's smile just as brightly.

"What a wonderful party, dear."

Turning, Janet took in her new friend—a woman who already seemed lighter and happier. "Audrey, you made it."

Audrey opened her arms for a welcoming hug. "I did. And I wanted you to know that I heard from that nice Stacy Hartman. She told me that she made her grandfather's exhibit conditional on revealing Mama as the true creator of *Need It? Grow It.* And the sponsors have agreed." Audrey put a hand to her chest, clearly still surprised by everything that had transpired over the past week. "Mama's work is going to be seen, Janet. By thousands of people. I suppose that technically, it already has. But now the people who see it will know that my mama was behind it."

"I wish she could be here to see it. She never knew."

"God knew, dear. And now we do too, thanks to you."

"And soon, *everyone* will know," Janet said. "When the news breaks."

Audrey shook her head. "I've told the organizers I simply want Mama's name to be shown alongside the sketches and the completed film. Those who really pay attention will notice the change. If they don't, then they don't."

"But, Audrey—"

"I don't want this to be sensationalized in any way, Janet. Stacy loved her grandfather the way I loved Mama. Turning this into some big, awful thing is no better than what happened in the first place."

Janet studied Audrey closely. "You are an amazing woman. You do know that, right?"

"I don't know about that," Audrey said, blushing. "Two wrongs don't make a right. I know the truth now. Mama's work touched and encouraged people at a time when that was sorely needed. That's enough for me."

Her cheeks still pink, Audrey ducked her head and said, so low Janet almost missed it, "I'm also looking forward to seeing if it's actually *not* too late to chase my own childhood dream."

"Wait. You mean you're going to start drawing for real?" Janet squawked, loudly enough to turn several pairs of eyes in their direction.

"I'm going to send some of the drawings I've stashed over the years to some agents who represent children's book illustrators."

Janet threw her arms around Audrey again, her excitement almost too great to bear. "Audrey, I am so, so glad to hear that. And I know in my heart that your mother would be too."

"I'm sure of it. And I have you to thank for it." Audrey hefted a gift bag Janet hadn't noticed before. "I have a present."

"You didn't need to do that, Audrey. We said no gifts, remember?"

"This one isn't just for Ian, my friend," Audrey said, handing it over with a mysterious smile. "This one is for both of you."

Puzzled, Janet made her way through the crowd of friends and loved ones who'd descended on the café to help her honor the man she loved, the man she would grow old with. When she reached him, she tapped his shoulder and greeted him with the smile he always stirred inside her soul.

"Happy birthday, my love," she said, holding out the bag. "This is a present from Audrey, for both of us."

He reached into the bag and withdrew the contents. "Oh, Janet," he murmured, gazing at the framed picture. "This is perfect."

"It is?"

"Yes." He held out the gift so she could see it better.

She drew in her breath at the drawing of her older self sitting on a bench with an older Ian and overlooking the fields of the Scottish countryside, their hands entwined. A rainbow stretched across a breathtakingly blue sky overhead. "It's…" She trailed off, at a loss for words.

"It's the most perfect gift anyone could have given us," Ian said, his voice thick with emotion. "I look forward to celebrating our fiftieth year together on this same bench, my love, in this same spot, with your hand in mine. Forever and always."

Dear Reader,

When I was asked to be part of the Whistle Stop Café Mystery series, I was thrilled for a few reasons. One, of course, is that I love writing mysteries. Two, I was intrigued by the challenge of crafting a contemporary story with ties to World War II. And finally, I knew it would give me another excuse to visit, even if mentally, with my late uncle Ray, a proud WWII veteran who passed away in 2016 at the age of 96. I think about him often—his smile, his mischievousness, his voice, his positive attitude, and his patriotism, but in researching that time period for *Somewhere Over the Rainbow,* I felt as if he was with me, guiding my searches and helping to satisfy my curiosity.

When I hear the term *The Greatest Generation* used to describe those who grew up during WWII, it is not hard to understand why. The sacrifices they made both overseas and at home, the way men and women of all ethnicities, races, and creeds pitched in for a common goal, and the way they moved through hardship with grace is something that really speaks to me.

Uncle Ray didn't graduate from high school in his teen years. The youngest of twelve children, it was more important for him to work and serve his country. Still, when the war was over and he had his own family, he worked hard despite that lack of education. He kept a roof over his family's head and food on the table, and he was always a positive light with a strong faith.

I'd like to think that he would have enjoyed reading *Somewhere Over the Rainbow*, just as I hope you all did.

Best wishes,
Laura Bradford

PS Fun Fact: Uncle Ray went on to get his high school diploma at the age of eighty-two, thanks to a special program for WWII vets in New York.

ABOUT the AUTHOR

While spending a rainy afternoon at a friend's house as a child, Laura Bradford fell in love with writing over a stack of blank paper, a box of crayons, and a freshly sharpened number-two pencil. From that moment forward, she never wanted to do or be anything other than an author (besides a mom).

Laura has nearly forty books in print, including Amish-based women's fiction novels and cozy mysteries with a variety of fun, everyday sleuths. When she's not writing, Laura loves to bake, travel, and advocate for those living with multiple sclerosis.

A GLIMPSE *of the* PAST

*T*oday, when we think of animation, we tend to think of movies with a prince or princess as the leading character or a cute animal that teaches us about friendship or reaching one's potential. But during World War II, animation was used in very different ways, thanks to animators like Walt Disney.

Disney and the United States Army came together in the wake of the Pearl Harbor attack to make animated films with specific messages for soldiers and for those on the home front. The films made for the soldiers centered around training and education on a variety of wartime topics, while those made for the general public sought to boost morale, strengthen support, encourage the purchase of war bonds, to serve as a reminder to pay taxes, and to calm fears about food shortages.

Some of today's best-known animated characters first became popular or saw a huge jump in their popularity because of their appearances in wartime films geared toward those on the home front. Some of these iconic characters and the messages they helped to convey include:

- Disney's Donald Duck listens carefully to the radio in the short film, *New Spirit*, as it reminds him how important it is that he pay his taxes and explains how to fill out his tax form.

- Donald is seen again in another film, *Spirit of '43*. In that one, he is torn between spending his money in frivolous ways or saving it to pay his taxes and thus aid in the war effort.
- Minnie Mouse and Mickey's dog, Pluto, starred in *Out of the Frying Pan into the Firing Line* to let people know how important it was to recycle their cooking grease. Doing so helped the country make explosives.

Animated films shown to soldiers were a bit darker, with themes ranging from flying and repairing aircraft to operating and cleaning tanks and just about everything in between. Some films with a character known as Private Snafu showed, by example, how *not* to conduct oneself on the battlefield or while on a break in a foreign country.

Animated short films shown in theaters were an effective and entertaining way to unite the country during the Second World War.

FROM the HOME-FRONT KITCHEN

Apple Cinnamon Muffins

Yield: 12 muffins

Ingredients:

Muffins:

2 cups all-purpose flour + 2
    teaspoons

1½ teaspoons baking powder

½ teaspoon kosher salt

2 teaspoons ground cinnamon,
    + ½ teaspoon

2 cups diced apples

½ cup butter, softened

1 cup brown sugar

2 large eggs

2 teaspoons vanilla extract

½ cup milk

Topping:

½ cup butter

¼ cup brown sugar

2 tablespoons ground cinnamon

Directions:

1. Preheat oven to 375. Grease muffin tin with butter and dust with flour.

2. Sift together 2 cups flour, baking powder, salt, and 2 teaspoons cinnamon in medium bowl. Set aside.

3. Mix 2 teaspoons flour with ½ teaspoon cinnamon in bowl large enough to hold diced apples. Toss diced apples with flour/cinnamon mixture. Set aside.

4. Cream butter and sugar until light and fluffy, about 2 to 3 minutes. Add eggs, one at a time, mixing well in between. Add vanilla.

5. Gently fold in flour mixture, alternating with milk. Stir until just combined. Fold in diced apples.

6. Scoop mixture into muffin tin, filling each space about ⅔ full. Bake about 30 minutes or until a toothpick inserted in the middle comes out clean.

7. While muffins are baking, prepare topping. Melt butter in a bowl large enough to dip the tops of the muffins in. Mix brown sugar and cinnamon in a separate bowl, also large enough for dipping.

8. When muffins are done, remove them from oven and allow them to cool for a few minutes in the muffin tin. Remove each muffin and dip the top into the melted butter and then into the cinnamon sugar mixture. Place on a plate to finish cooling.

*Read on for a sneak peek of another exciting book
in the* Whistle Stop Café Mysteries *series!*

DOWN FORGET-
ME-NOT LANE

BY LESLIE GOULD

"R eady?" Debbie Albright knelt beside Ray Zink's wheelchair.

He turned toward her, his eyes misty under his dark-blue garrison cap fringed by his snow-white hair. Was he thinking of that day eighty years ago when he'd rushed onto Omaha Beach as a nineteen-year-old in June of 1944? Would the early Thursday afternoon ceremony be too much for this precious, nearly ninety-nine-year-old veteran and dear, dear friend?

The guests had already gathered outside the depot for the ceremony to honor Ray, but Debbie would make an excuse for him if needed. "Are you all right?" she whispered.

Ray squared his shoulders under the army dress jacket that hung loosely on his frail frame. "Absolutely. Let's go."

Debbie stood, stepped behind his chair, and then pushed Ray through the open doors of the depot, past pots of red and purple petunias, and out to the parking lot, where a podium, white tent, and chairs waited. Ray had been movie-star handsome as a young man, and it was still evident in his features. But it was his kind and humble disposition that drew people to him, and at least part of why the town was eager to honor him in this way.

The warm June sunshine welcomed them, along with newscaster Jonathon Bell. Debbie had invited him from Columbus. His cameraman, who wore jeans and a T-shirt, filmed as Jonathon grinned and said to Ray, "I'd love to interview you after the ceremony, if that's all right with you."

Ray gave him a thumbs-up. Debbie smiled and kept pushing the chair.

A hundred or more citizens of Dennison were already seated in the shade of the tent, along with Ray's younger sister, Gayle, and his niece, Trudy, who had also come from Columbus.

As Debbie wheeled Ray into the tent—decorated with red, white, and blue bunting and twinkle lights—the attendees rose to their feet. When Debbie stopped his chair at the front, everyone began to clap. Debbie's eyes filled with tears.

Greg Connor, chairman of the chamber of commerce and a good friend of Debbie's, stepped to the podium and faced Ray as the crowd stopped clapping and sat down. "Welcome, Ray." Greg's blue eyes seemed even more brilliant than usual as he met Ray's gaze. "Thank you for your service to our country eighty years ago and for your continued service to our town in the years since." Greg's grandfather had died in World War II, decades before Greg was born. He respected Ray all the more because of it.

Greg addressed the audience. "We're gathered here today to honor Ray Zink, but also to remember the more than four hundred thousand

American soldiers who died during World War II and the sixteen million who served during the war."

Debbie's heart swelled at Greg's words. She'd learned so much about World War II, both on the home front and in the war zones, since she'd moved back home to Dennison.

"First we'll hear from Kim Smith, curator of our museum," Greg said, "and then from Ray himself. And I just found out that we have a couple of special guests who've traveled here to honor Ray today also."

Debbie wondered who they could be. She'd helped plan the event and hadn't heard about any special guests. She positioned Ray's wheelchair in front of the podium, facing the audience, then sat near him in the first row of chairs as Kim stepped to the podium.

Kim talked about Dennison during World War II and the many young men who enlisted in the military or were drafted and then sent overseas. "Ray is the last remaining World War II veteran living in Dennison," she said, "which makes him our very own treasure. We don't take his service nor his long life for granted. Not only did he help liberate Europe from the Nazis and preserve the free world, but he's helped to preserve our own history ever since, while also assisting veterans who returned from Korea, Vietnam, the Gulf, Iraq, and Afghanistan."

Debbie didn't know that Ray had helped other veterans, but she wasn't surprised. He was one of the kindest and most generous people she had ever met.

Kim gave more information about Ray's service. He had landed on Omaha Beach during the D-Day and Normandy Campaign then made his way through northern France. He'd taken part in the beginning of the liberation of the Netherlands, where he'd been wounded and recovered in a hospital in England. Then he had been assigned to a unit that worked with the British Royal Engineers to clear land mines.

"He played a part in freeing the island of Guernsey in the Channel Islands and then was injured a second time in 1945. After recovering again in a British hospital, he returned home to the US." She went on to list his medals, including a Purple Heart and a Bronze Star.

Jonathon Bell's cameraman was off to the side, filming the speakers while Jonathon sat in an aisle chair, scrolling on his phone, which seemed odd to Debbie.

"We can never fully express our gratitude for everything you've done," Kim told Ray. "But we hope you feel appreciated. Now, as I understand it, you want to say a few words." She handed him the microphone.

He started by saying, "Thank you, Kim. I'm honored to be here today. Every morning, I wake up grateful for another day on this earth and in this town. I've been blessed beyond measure. I don't know why the Good Lord saw fit to save me twice during the war when so many never returned, but I haven't taken a minute of the last eighty years for granted. I want to be worthy of this life that the Lord has given me."

Debbie made eye contact with Gayle, who was sitting in the front row. Both women had to swipe away tears.

Ray went on to thank Greg, Kim, and Debbie for the ceremony, and then he honored the men he'd served with. "All of those who returned and all of those who didn't are always in my memories." He patted his chest. "And in my heart. Thank you again, everyone."

He passed the microphone to Greg while everyone applauded.

Greg announced, "Speaking of the men Ray served with, we have Ohio State Representative Heather Clark here today." Ray stirred as Greg continued. "She's the daughter of Representative Leland Clark, who passed away nine years ago. He served with Ray in Holland and on Guernsey." He gestured toward the back of the crowd. "Representative Clark, please come forward."

A woman who wore a navy pencil skirt and matching jacket started down the middle aisle, with a leather bag over her shoulder. She appeared to be in her late fifties or early sixties and wore her auburn hair shoulder length. She was followed by a young woman who seemed to be in her late teens, with straight red hair falling over one side of her face.

Heather Clark beamed at Ray and then accepted the microphone from Greg. "Thank you, Mr. Connor, for your kindness in having us here today." She put an arm around the young woman. "This is my niece, Ruby Clark, who is also here to honor Ray Zink."

Ruby gave a shy wave before her aunt continued.

"My father talked about Ray Zink a lot, because he was Ray's sergeant," Heather said. "When I found out that Ray was being honored today, I knew Ruby and I had to come." She took a picture frame out of her bag and held it up. "This sat on my father's desk until the day he died. It's a photo of him with Ray on Guernsey in June of 1945. They both look so full of hope and determination in spite of everything they'd already seen and been through." She turned to Ray. "I've made copies of the photo for myself and Ruby. I want you to have this one."

Heather handed the microphone back to Greg and approached Ray.

Ray took the photo in one hand and Heather's free hand in the other. "Thank you," he said, his voice trembling with emotion. "Thank you for this picture and for coming. I remember Leland with fondness. I hope you can stay for the reception."

"I wouldn't miss it," Heather assured him. "I hope we'll have time to chat."

Ray let go of Heather's hand and beckoned to Ruby. She stepped to his side and took his hand.

"I'm pleased to meet you, Ruby," Ray told her. "Thank you for coming."

She gave him a small smile, ducking her head so that her long hair swung forward to hide more of her face.

"We'll see you at the reception," Heather said.

The audience clapped, and Heather and Ruby started toward the back, where a young man in a black suit stood.

"Thank you, Representative Clark and Ruby. What a nice surprise to have you here today," Greg said. "We have one more surprise for you, Ray. Oliver Godfrey has come all the way from Guernsey to honor you."

The crowd murmured in surprise.

Ray turned to Debbie with wide eyes. "What's happening? Should I know that name?"

"I'm not sure," she answered.

A short, thin man in corduroy pants and a brown plaid jacket made his way toward Greg. He had gray hair and appeared to be in his midsixties or so. A leather satchel was strapped across his chest.

"Oliver has been searching for Ray for the last decade and finally tracked him down a month ago. When he found out we were having a ceremony today to honor Ray, he traveled all this way to be here." Greg handed Oliver the microphone.

The man seemed overwhelmed for a moment but then turned to Ray and said, "My mother was Adele Martin, the little girl you saved in June of 1945. I can't believe I've finally found you."

The crowd gasped. Ray reached for Debbie, and she took his hand, her own shaking as much as his.

"My mother was ten years old," Oliver continued. "Her father had been in the service since 1939, and he was scheduled to arrive in St. Peter Port that day. Her grandmother was ill, so she was delayed getting down to the docks. She took a shortcut and began running through a field toward the road, but—unknown to her—a live mine was in that field. Ray Zink risked his own life to save hers, injuring himself in the process." Oliver paused a moment and then said, "I grew up hearing stories about Ray Zink. My mother owed her life to him, and so do I. He's a true American hero."

The crowd sat in shocked silence for a moment. But then Greg began to clap, and others did too. Soon the entire audience was standing, clapping, and cheering. And Debbie was swiping tears from her eyes once again.

The ceremony wasn't what she'd planned—but it couldn't have been better. And Ray deserved every second of it.

Half an hour later, Ray sat in the lobby of the depot as the last of the crowd filed by to shake his hand and then enjoy cookies made by Janet Shaw, who co-owned the Whistle Stop Café with Debbie. Tables were set up in the lobby, and more people than usual were squeezed into the café. The museum was open, and part of the crowd drifted that way.

Once everyone had greeted Ray, Jonathon Bell interviewed him, asking a few follow-up questions about what Ray had said during the celebration.

After he finished the interview, Jonathon said, "I'm fascinated by World War II memorabilia and have been collecting it for years."

"What made you interested in it?" Ray asked.

"I have a great-uncle who served. He didn't have children, so I inherited his uniform twenty years ago when he passed away. After that, I bought more World War II items at estate sales and that sort of thing. Now I buy things online." He held up his phone. "In fact, I bid on a jacket a few minutes ago." Before Ray could respond, Jonathon shook his hand. "Thanks for your time, as well as for your service. I'm going to go walk through the museum and then leave. We have to get back to Columbus to film a high school graduation. Five generations in one family have graduated from the same school."

"Nice," Debbie said. "Thank you again."

Jonathon gave her a nod.

Debbie pushed Ray's chair to the table where Gayle sat with Trudy, and grabbed a cup of coffee and a cookie for him.

Then Debbie went into the café to check on Janet to see if she needed any help. "I've got this under control," Janet said from behind the counter where she was making a mocha. "Go mingle."

Debbie headed toward Ray's table but stopped to speak with Greg first. "When did you find out that Heather Clark and Oliver Godfrey were here?"

"Not until right before the ceremony began. Otherwise, I would have told you. Heather and her assistant found me about ten minutes before. They'd left a message at the chamber, but I missed it."

Debbie nodded at the young man in the suit who stood with Heather and Ruby. "Is that her assistant?"

"Yes," Greg said. "He's a recent college graduate. He's working for a year before he goes to law school. And then Oliver arrived a few minutes before we started."

Where was Oliver? Debbie glanced around the lobby and found him talking with her parents. No doubt they had approached him. They always formed a welcome wagon.

"Oliver's arrival really shocked me," Greg said. "It's one thing to have the daughter of someone Ray served with come in from Columbus. But to have Oliver come all the way from the United Kingdom—that's nothing short of fantastic."

"Ray was obviously touched," Debbie said. "It's hard for me to picture someone running across a field of land mines to save a little girl. But it's completely in line with who Ray is, so if I could see anyone doing that, it would be him."

Greg shuddered. "I can't imagine being in that situation. And the closer my boys get to the age Ray was when he enlisted, the more real it all seems." Jaxon and Julian were in their midteens, and Ray had been newly eighteen when he'd been sent overseas.

Heather and Ruby approached Ray's table. Debbie excused herself to Greg and met them there, introducing them to Gayle and Trudy.

"How lovely that you were able to come," Gayle said to the representative. "We live in your district, but I had no idea your father served with my brother. What a special connection."

Heather smiled. "I can't tell you how much I wish I'd known Ray was in Ohio. Dad would have loved to reconnect. To think they were so close but never saw each other again." She shook her head. "It's such a shame."

"How did you find out about the celebration?" Debbie asked Heather.

"Last night on the news, when Jonathon mentioned that he was coming here today." Obviously, Heather was on a first-name basis with the newscaster. "He mentioned that Ray Zink landed on Omaha Beach, was injured in Holland, and cleared mines in the Channel Islands. That was Dad's exact route. I had a hunch they must have served together, and Jonathon confirmed it this morning when he texted me a photo of Ray as a soldier. It was the same young man in Dad's photo. Ruby and I packed up and hit the road—and my assistant, Graham, was able to join us here."

"Wonderful," Debbie said. "I'm so glad you were able to make it on such short notice."

"I'm really missing Dad today, but this is helping." Heather gestured to the medals on Ray's jacket. "One thing I don't understand is why Dad never got a Purple Heart. Weren't all soldiers who were injured in action by the enemy supposed to receive one?"

"That's right, as long as they required treatment by a medical officer at the time of the injury," Ray said. "But there were all sorts of paperwork snags. When it hadn't come through after several months, Leland said he'd petition the army to award him one after the war."

"He said it never arrived."

"Oh, that's too bad. It would be nice for you to have it now, to remember your father and Ruby's grandfather."

Ruby blushed. She really was a shy one.

Out of the corner of her eye, Debbie spotted Oliver Godfrey shaking her mom's hand and then her dad's before making his way toward Ray's table. When he reached them, Debbie introduced herself to Oliver and then introduced him to Heather and her group.

"Pleased to meet you," Heather said. "Dad always told us he'd rescued a little girl from a minefield on Guernsey. Were there two girls who were rescued?"

"I've never heard of another rescue like my mother's, but that doesn't mean there wasn't one. I do have some questions for Ray though."

"Go ahead," Ray replied.

"How did you manage to cross the field without setting off any mines?"

"It was the last mine in the field," Ray said. "The engineers had partly dismantled it and then stopped for lunch."

Heather crossed her arms. "I'm sure it was Dad who rescued the girl. I heard the story my entire life."

A chatting passerby bumped into Ray's chair. Ray jerked, and his coffee spilled onto his military jacket, including his medals. "Oh, dear," he said. "Look what I've done."

Debbie grabbed a napkin and began dabbing at the coffee as Carl Miller, who was buying the dry-cleaning business in town from his older brother, paused at her side. "Let me take that to the shop. I'll clean it right away and have it back to you by morning."

Jonathon, Heather, and Oliver all watched as Debbie helped Ray remove his jacket. The cameraman stood behind Jonathon with the camera still on his shoulder.

Carl accepted the jacket from Debbie. "Stop by first thing in the morning. This will be ready by then."

"I will," she answered. "Thank you."

Carl nodded and hurried away.

Ray sighed. "I think I should go home and rest. This has all been wonderful, but I'm tired."

Trudy stood and helped her mother rise. "We'll give you a ride back to Good Shepherd, Uncle Ray."

"Will we see you again?" Heather asked him.

"You're welcome to join me at the retirement center for dinner." Ray shifted his gaze to Oliver. "You too, Mr. Godfrey. I'd love to chat with both of you more. Dinner starts at five. We're having meatballs and gravy, with apple pie for dessert."

"We'll be there," Heather said.

"So will I." Oliver smiled.

"Would you come for dinner too?" Ray asked Debbie as Trudy stepped behind his chair. "And invite Janet and Ian—I think Ian and Oliver might hit it off." Ian had emigrated from Scotland as a boy.

"Absolutely." She smiled down at him as he patted her hand.

Trudy pushed him to the exit with Gayle walking beside them. Ahead of them, Carl stepped out of the depot and turned toward his shop downtown, carrying Ray's jacket over his arm.

Debbie turned back to look at their surprise guests. When she saw the pinched expression on Heather's face, she gave Ray Zink credit for not only being kind and generous. He was also smart. She was willing to bet that Ian being from Scotland wasn't the only reason he'd asked for their presence at dinner.

While you are waiting for the next fascinating story in the Whistle Stop Café Mysteries, check out some other Guideposts mystery series!

SAVANNAH SECRETS

Welcome to Savannah, Georgia, a picture-perfect Southern city known for its manicured parks, moss-covered oaks, and antebellum architecture. Walk down one of the cobblestone streets, and you'll come upon Magnolia Investigations. It is here where two friends have joined forces to unravel some of Savannah's deepest secrets. Tag along as clues are exposed, red herrings discarded, and thrilling surprises revealed. Find inspiration in the special bond between Meredith Bellefontaine and Julia Foley. Cheer the friends on as they listen to their hearts and rely on their faith to solve each new case that comes their way.

The Hidden Gate
A Fallen Petal
Double Trouble
Whispering Bells
Where Time Stood Still
The Weight of Years
Willful Transgressions

Season's Meetings

Southern Fried Secrets

The Greatest of These

Patterns of Deception

The Waving Girl

Beneath a Dragon Moon

Garden Variety Crimes

Meant for Good

A Bone to Pick

Honeybees & Legacies

True Grits

Sapphire Secret

Jingle Bell Heist

Buried Secrets

A Puzzle of Pearls

Facing the Facts

Resurrecting Trouble

Forever and a Day

MYSTERIES of MARTHA'S VINEYARD

Priscilla Latham Grant has inherited a lighthouse! So with not much more than a strong will and a sore heart, the recent widow says goodbye to her lifelong Kansas home and heads to the quaint and historic island of Martha's Vineyard, Massachusetts. There, she comes face-to-face with adventures, which include her trusty canine friend, Jake, three delightful cousins she didn't know she had, and Gerald O'Bannon, a handsome Coast Guard captain—plus head-scratching mysteries that crop up with surprising regularity.

A Light in the Darkness
Like a Fish Out of Water
Adrift
Maiden of the Mist
Making Waves
Don't Rock the Boat
A Port in the Storm
Thicker Than Water
Swept Away
Bridge Over Troubled Waters
Smoke on the Water
Shifting Sands
Shark Bait
Seascape in Shadows

Storm Tide
Water Flows Uphill
Catch of the Day
Beyond the Sea
Wider Than an Ocean
Sheeps Passing in the Night
Sail Away Home
Waves of Doubt
Lifeline
Flotsam & Jetsam
Just Over the Horizon

MIRACLES & MYSTERIES of MERCY HOSPITAL

Four talented women from very different walks of life witness the miracles happening around them at Mercy Hospital and soon become fast friends. Join Joy Atkins, Evelyn Perry, Anne Mabry, and Shirley Bashore as, together, they solve the puzzling mysteries that arise at this Charleston, South Carolina, historic hospital—rumored to be under the protection of a guardian angel. Come along as our quartet of faithful friends solve mysteries, stumble upon a few of the hospital's hidden and forgotten passageways, and discover historical treasures along the way! This fast-paced series is filled with inspiration, adventure, mystery, delightful humor, and loads of Southern charm!

Where Mercy Begins
Prescription for Mystery
Angels Watching Over Me
A Change of Art
Conscious Decisions
Surrounded by Mercy
Broken Bonds
Mercy's Healing
To Heal a Heart

A Cross to Bear

Merciful Secrecy

Sunken Hopes

Hair Today, Gone Tomorrow

Pain Relief

Redeemed by Mercy

A Genius Solution

A Hard Pill to Swallow

Ill at Ease

'Twas the Clue Before Christmas

A NOTE FROM the EDITORS

We hope you enjoyed another exciting volume in the Whistle Stop Café Mysteries series, published by Guideposts. For over seventy-five years, Guideposts, a nonprofit organization, has been driven by a vision of a world filled with hope. We aspire to be the voice of a trusted friend, a friend who makes you feel more hopeful and connected.

By making a purchase from Guideposts, you join our community in touching millions of lives, inspiring them to believe that all things are possible through faith, hope, and prayer. Your continued support allows us to provide uplifting resources to those in need. Whether through our communities, websites, apps, or publications, we inspire our audiences, bring them together, and comfort, uplift, entertain, and guide them. Visit us at guideposts.org to learn more.

We would love to hear from you. Write us at Guideposts, P.O. Box 5815, Harlan, Iowa 51593 or call us at (800) 932-2145. Did you love *Somewhere Over the Rainbow*? Leave a review for this product on guideposts.org/shop. Your feedback helps others in our community find relevant products.

Find inspiration, find faith, find Guideposts.

Shop our best sellers and favorites at
guideposts.org/shop

Or scan the QR code to go directly to our Shop

Find more inspiring stories in these best-loved Guideposts fiction series!

Mysteries of Lancaster County

Follow the Classen sisters as they unravel clues and uncover hidden secrets in Mysteries of Lancaster County. As you get to know these women and their friends, you'll see how God brings each of them together for a fresh start in life.

Secrets of Wayfarers Inn

Retired schoolteachers find themselves owners of an old warehouse-turned-inn that is filled with hidden passages, buried secrets, and stunning surprises that will set them on a course to puzzling mysteries from the Underground Railroad.

Tearoom Mysteries Series

Mix one stately Victorian home, a charming lakeside town in Maine, and two adventurous cousins with a passion for tea and hospitality. Add a large scoop of intriguing mystery, and sprinkle generously with faith, family, and friends, and you have the recipe for *Tearoom Mysteries*.

Ordinary Women of the Bible

Richly imagined stories—based on facts from the Bible—have all the plot twists and suspense of a great mystery, while bringing you fascinating insights on what it was like to be a woman living in the ancient world.

To learn more about these books, visit Guideposts.org/Shop